SOCIAL MEDIA ADVERTISIN G

FINANCIAL SUCCESS GUIDE HOW TO MANAGE RISK AND Build Your PERSONAL BRAND ON SOCIAL MEDIA SITES LIKE FACEBOOK, INSTAGRAM, AND LINKEDIN TO to EXPAND YOUR BUSINESS.

RICHARD N. WILLIAMS

TABLE OF
CONTENTS

INTRODUCT ION

In the unique domain of computerized promoting, Emily, a carefully prepared advertiser with a propensity for development, wound up exploring the steadily changing scene of online entertainment publicizing. Equipped with a dream to upset procedures on stages like Facebook, Instagram, and LinkedIn, she left on an excursion that wouldn't just rethink achievement yet in addition embody the flexibility of the human soul.

Emily's enlivening came during a promoting gathering where she saw the extraordinary force of a top notch online entertainment crusade. Enlivened, she imagined a future where organizations could associate with their crowd in significant ways, rising above the regular limits of promoting.

Energized by this motivation, Emily dug profound into grasping the complexities of every stage. She looked at user behavior, trends, and successful campaigns to look for patterns that could be used.

Facebook, with its different client base, turned into a material for narrating. While LinkedIn's professional aura required a strategic approach, Instagram's visual appeal beckoned for creative expression.

In her quest for greatness, Emily experienced difficulties that tried her grit. Calculations changed, patterns advanced, and buyer inclinations moved. However, rather than surrendering to the vulnerability, Emily embraced it as a chance for transformation. She encouraged her team to stay ahead of the curve by cultivating a culture of continuous learning.

Perceiving that development comes from cooperation, Emily encouraged organizations with powerhouses and thought forerunners in the business. These partnerships improved the validity of the missions as well as worked with a more credible association with the crowd. The reverberation of these organizations reverberated across stages, intensifying the effect of the publicizing systems.

Emily's flexibility genuinely sparkled during a vital second when an unexpected calculation update took steps to disturb their carefully created crusades. As opposed to respecting alarm, Emily accumulated her group for a meeting to generate new ideas.

They recalibrated their methodology, investigating new elements and functionalities that the refreshed calculations inclined toward. This rescued their continuous missions as well as situated them as trailblazers in adjusting to change.

The core of Emily's prosperity lay in her capacity to refine brands through narrating. She urged her group to go past the traditional attempt to sell something, encouraging them to create stories that resonated with the crowd on an individual level. This change in approach changed notices from nosy interferences to convincing stories that clients eagerly drew in with and shared.

As the missions picked up speed, Emily observed the investigation with an insightful eye. She used the data as a compass to optimize strategies for maximum impact. A/B testing turned into a foundation of their methodology, permitting them to tweak each component of the missions and uncover experiences that powered constant improvement.

The genuine proportion of Emily's prosperity, nonetheless, lay in the measurements as well as in the narratives that unfurled past the computerized domain. Businesses that had previously struggled to assert themselves online now thrive. Business people tracked down new roads to associate with their crowd, and new companies changed into industry disruptors.

Considering her excursion, Emily understood that the substance of virtual entertainment promoting went past calculations and investigation. It was tied in with understanding the heartbeat of a brand and making an interpretation of it into a language that resounded with the crowd. It was tied in with embracing change with enduring versatility and review difficulties as any open doors for development.

Eventually, Emily's story isn't only one of progress in the advanced advertising circle; it's a demonstration of the extraordinary force of development, versatility, and the human soul. Through her relentless obligation to reclassifying web-based entertainment publicizing, Emily raised her profession as well as propelled an age of advertisers to embrace change and specialty crusades that rose above the computerized scene.

Overview of Social Media Advertising

Modern marketing strategies now include social media advertising, which has revolutionized how businesses connect with their target audience. The evolution of social media advertising, its advantages, obstacles, and emerging trends are examined in depth in this overview.

Development of Web-based Entertainment Promoting:

The advertising landscape has been altered by the rise of social media platforms like Facebook, Twitter, Instagram, and LinkedIn. From the beginning, these stages were principally channels for individual correspondence. In any case, perceiving their immense client bases and commitment levels, organizations started to investigate them as promoting mediums.

The advancement of virtual entertainment promotion can be followed back to the presentation of Facebook Advertisements in 2007. This obviously a defining moment, permitting promoters to arrive at explicit socioeconomics in light of clients' inclinations, ways of behaving, and socioeconomics.

The progress of Facebook Promotions prepared for different stages to foster their publicizing models, making a dynamic and serious market.

Advantages of Web-based Entertainment Promoting:

Designated Promoting: One of the essential benefits of web-based entertainment publicizing is the capacity to target explicit crowd fragments. Sponsors can characterize their interest group in light of socioeconomics, interests, online way of behaving, and area, guaranteeing that their messages contact the ideal individuals.

Commitment and Association: Online entertainment stages give a one of a kind chance to brands to straightforwardly draw in with their crowd. Notices can produce likes, offers, remarks, and direct messages, encouraging a feeling of local area and brand dedication.

Cost-Effective: Contrasted with customary promoting channels, virtual entertainment publicizing can be more financially savvy. Promoters can draw spending plan lines and pay-per-snap or pay-per-impression, guaranteeing that they get an incentive for their speculation.

Examination and Estimation: Online entertainment stages offer powerful investigation instruments that empower sponsors to follow the presentation of their missions. Measurements like reach, commitment, navigate rates, and changes give important experiences, permitting sponsors to refine their techniques.

Challenges in Web-based Entertainment Publicizing:

Competition and Saturation: As additional organizations perceive the capability of virtual entertainment promoting, stages have become

6

immersed with content. Ferocious contest can make it provoking for promoters to stick out and catch crowd consideration.

Changing the algorithm: Web-based entertainment calculations continually develop, influencing the perceivability of notices. Calculation changes can influence the natural reach of content, making it fundamental for promoters to adjust and remain informed about stage refreshes.

Promotion Exhaustion: Crowds might encounter promotion weakness when presented to tedious or superfluous substances. To battle this, publicists should consistently revive their imaginative materials and designer messages to reverberate with their main interest group.

Privacy issues: Advertising practices on social media have come under increased scrutiny as a result of the increased awareness of data privacy issues. Publicists should explore protection guidelines and discuss straightforwardly with clients to fabricate trust.

Arising Patterns in Online Entertainment Publicizing:

Video Predominance: Video content keeps on overwhelming web-based entertainment stages. Short-structure recordings, live streams, and intuitive substance are acquiring fame, giving sponsors better approaches to draw in crowds.

Temporary Content: Advertisers can now create time-sensitive and immersive campaigns thanks to the rise of ephemeral content like Instagram and Snapchat stories.

Force to be reckoned with Advertising: Working together with powerhouses has turned into a strong technique for web-based entertainment promoting. Powerhouses can assist brands with contacting a bigger and more designated crowd, utilizing their believability and association with supporters.

Increased Reality (AR) and Computer generated Reality (VR): Social media advertising gains an interactive and immersive dimension by incorporating AR and VR technologies. Brands can make novel encounters for clients, upgrading commitment and brand review.

advertising on social media has developed into a dynamic and crucial component of modern marketing strategies. While it offers various advantages, publicists should explore difficulties, for example, expanded contests, calculation changes, and security concerns. By keeping up to date with arising patterns and utilizing the assorted elements of online entertainment stages, organizations can make significant missions that resonate with their crowd and drive results.

Importance in the Digital Age

The idea of importance has undergone a significant shift in the digital age, affecting various aspects of our personal and professional lives. The fast headway of innovation has reshaped the manner in which we impart as well as reclassified the meaning of data, associations, and abilities in this interconnected time.

One of the key viewpoints where significance becomes the dominant focal point is in the domain of data. We are surrounded by an overwhelming amount of data from a variety of sources in the digital age. The capacity to perceive, channel, and focus on data has become essential. Significance, in this unique circumstance, lies in the ability of data on the board — knowing what to assimilate, what to dispose of, and what to follow up on. In a world overflowed with information, the ability to recognize signals from clamor is a significant resource.

In addition, the advanced age has raised the significance of the network. Interpersonal organizations, online networks, and texting stages have woven a trap of interconnectedness that rises above topographical limits. The capacity to construct and support significant connections online has turned into a fundamental expertise. Significance, in this specific circumstance, is credited to one's web-based presence, abilities to organize, and the development of a computerized persona that lines up with individual and expert objectives.

In the expert scene, the significance of versatility and consistent learning has flooded. The computerized age is described by fast mechanical development, and remaining important requires a pledge to progressing training. The significance, thusly, lies in the amassing of information as well as in the capacity to quickly adjust to new apparatuses, stages, and techniques. In this unique climate, the ability to learn turns into a vital figure deciding one's expert achievement.

Additionally, the digital age has rethought the significance of skills. Specialized capability, advanced education, and capability in exploring computerized apparatuses are at this point not discretionary yet basic. The capacity to use innovation for efficiency, critical thinking, and development has turned into an essential in many fields. The acquisition and mastery of digital skills that enable individuals to thrive in a world that is becoming increasingly digitized is emphasized in this context.

In the computerized age, the idea of time has likewise seen a change in significance. With the speed increase of correspondence and the coming of constant coordinated effort devices, the capacity to oversee time productively has turned into a basic expertise. Significance is put on time usage methodologies, performing various tasks capacities, and the ability to focus on undertakings in a high speed, interconnected climate.

Network safety has turned into a fundamental worry in the computerized age, raising the significance of safeguarding individual and delicate data. With the rising recurrence and refinement of digital dangers, people and associations should focus on the execution of vigorous network safety measures. The significance of computerized security mindfulness, encryption methods, and secure internet based rehearsals couldn't possibly be more significant.

Also, the computerized age has intensified the significance of inventiveness and advancement. As computerization assumes control over routine errands, human creativity turns into a distinctive variable. The capacity to think imaginatively, take care of intricate issues, and imagine inventive arrangements is exceptionally esteemed. In a scene where innovation quickly develops, the significance of developing an imaginative outlook and cultivating development is critical for people and associations alike.

All in all, the computerized age has achieved a change in perspective by the way we see and focus on significance. The importance of information management, digital connectivity, adaptability, skill development, time management, cybersecurity, and creativity has grown in this era. Exploring the intricacies of the advanced scene expects people to embrace these viewpoints as well as to persistently develop and remain sensitive to the steadily changing elements of the computerized age.

Chapter 1 Platform- Specific Strategies

Making powerful web-based entertainment publicizing procedures includes grasping the novel elements of every stage. Your campaign's success can be significantly enhanced by tailoring your strategy to the particular demographics and strengths of platforms like Facebook, Instagram, Twitter, and LinkedIn.

Facebook:

Due to its large user base and extensive targeting options, Facebook continues to dominate social media advertising. Use the stage's high level segment focusing to arrive at explicit age gatherings, interests, and areas. Influence eye-getting visuals and brief duplicates in your promotions to catch clients' consideration as they look at their feeds. Integrating client produced content or intelligent components can increment commitment and make a feeling of local area around your image.

Also, exploit Facebook's powerful examination devices to follow key measurements, for example, navigate rates, transformation rates, and commitment. This information can illuminate changes in accordance with your technique continuously, guaranteeing ideal execution.

Instagram:

As an outwardly situated stage, Instagram blossoms with tastefully satisfying substance. By investing in high-quality images and imaginative storytelling, you can tailor your advertisements to the visual nature of the platform. Particularly, Instagram Stories provide a dynamic and engaging method for connecting with your audience. Use highlights like surveys, questions, and swipe-up connections to improve client commitment.

Team up with powerhouses to take advantage of their adherents and assemble genuineness around your image. Instagram's shopping highlights likewise give an open door to feature items straightforwardly inside the stage, smoothing out the client venture from disclosure to buy.

Twitter:

Twitter's quick moving and brief nature requires an alternate publicizing approach. Make convincing and concise duplicates that get consideration inside the stage's personality limit. Engage with hot topics to join conversations and use relevant hashtags to increase discoverability.

Advanced Tweets and Twitter Advertisements can intensify your range, particularly while focusing on unambiguous socioeconomics or interests. Carrying out sight and sound components like GIFs and recordings can make your substance hang out in the packed Twitter channel. Consistently screen and answer makes reference to and direct messages to encourage a feeling of local area and show client responsiveness.

LinkedIn:

LinkedIn takes special care of an expert crowd, making it an ideal stage for B2B promoting and proficient administrations. Create well-written, informative content that addresses the business requirements of your target audience directly. Use LinkedIn Promotions to arrive at explicit businesses, work titles, and company sizes.

Sharing idea administration content, like articles and whitepapers, can situate your image as an expert in your industry. Draw in with significant LinkedIn gatherings and partake in conversations to increment perceivability. Furthermore, utilizing worker promotion by empowering staff to share organization updates can intensify your arrival inside proficient organizations.

All in all, powerful web-based entertainment publicizing requires a nuanced comprehension of every stage's exceptional elements. Fitting your way to deal with the qualities and socioeconomics of Facebook, Instagram, Twitter, and LinkedIn can enhance your mission's effect. Routinely dissect execution measurements, adjust your methodology in light of experiences, and remain sensitive to developing patterns in online entertainment publicizing.

FACEBOOK
Advertising

Facebook promoting has turned into a foundation of computerized showcasing, giving organizations a strong stage to arrive at their interest group. With over 2.8 billion month to month dynamic clients, Facebook offers a broad and various client base for sponsors to associate with expected clients.

One of the critical qualities of Facebook publicizing lies in its strong focusing on choices. Promoters can limit their crowd in view of socio economics, interests, conduct, and even area. This degree of accuracy empowers organizations to fit their promotions to explicit customer portions, improving the probability of commitment and change.

The stage's promotion designs are one more critical part of its prosperity. From picture and video promotions to merry go round and slideshow designs, Facebook offers various choices to exhibit items or administrations imaginatively. Moreover, the as of late presented intuitive promotion designs, like increased reality promotions, permit brands to give vivid encounters, cultivating a more profound association with clients.

One striking element is the Facebook Pixel, a following instrument that assists organizations with estimating the viability of their publicizing endeavors. By dissecting client conduct on a site subsequent to tapping on a Facebook promotion, sponsors gain significant bits of knowledge into change rates, considering information driven enhancement. This criticism circle is instrumental in refining promotion methodologies, guaranteeing that advertising financial plans are allotted proficiently.

In addition, the algorithm of the platform is crucial to maximizing ad reach. Facebook's calculation uses AI to comprehend client inclinations, showing promotions to people who are bound to draw in with the substance. This dynamic focusing on component upgrades the general productivity of publicizing efforts, conveying improved results for organizations.

Facebook's Promotion Supervisor furnishes publicists with a brought together center point for making, making due, and investigating their missions.

The launching of advertisements is facilitated by this user-friendly interface, which provides a variety of customization options. Publicists can set financial plan limits, plan crusades, and A/B test different creatives to consistently upgrade execution.

An eminent strength of Facebook publicizing is its coordination with Instagram, which the stage procured in 2012. Promoters can flawlessly run crusades across the two stages, extending their scope to Instagram's outwardly situated client base. This incorporation empowers a strong brand presence across numerous web-based entertainment channels, improving generally showcasing viability.

Retargeting, one more impressive system presented by Facebook promoting, permits organizations to reconnect with clients who have recently collaborated with their site or application. By showing designated promotions to people who have shown interest yet didn't make a buy, publicists can support leads and guide them through the change channel.

Facebook likewise gives a set-up of examination instruments to exhaustively quantify promotion execution. Reach, engagement, click-through rate, and conversion tracking provide advertisers with a comprehensive comprehension of the effectiveness of their campaigns. This information driven approach enables organizations to settle on informed choices, upgrading their systems for improved results.

Regardless of its various benefits, Facebook publicizing isn't without challenges. Promotion weariness, where clients become inert to dull promotions, is a typical issue. To combat this, advertisers need to regularly update their creatives and try out new messages to keep their audience interested.

With increasing scrutiny of how platforms handle user data, privacy concerns have also emerged as a primary concern. Advertisers need to be aware of these concerns and make sure they adhere to changing privacy laws. Offsetting designated publicizing with client security is vital to keeping up with trust and believability.

All in all, Facebook publicizing has developed into a foundation of computerized promoting, offering a powerful stage for organizations to associate with their interest group. With its broad client base, high level focusing on choices, various promotion designs, and strong examination apparatuses, Facebook furnishes publicists with the devices they need to make successful and productive missions. While challenges like promotion weakness and protection concerns endure, the stage's ceaseless development and obligation to advancement make it a fundamental part of current showcasing techniques.

Targeting and Ad Formats

Focusing on and promoting designs are vital components in the realm of computerized publicizing, assuming an essential part in contacting the right crowd and boosting the viability of missions. As the computerized scene keeps on developing, sponsors are continually refining their methodologies to remain ahead in a cutthroat market.

Targeting: Accuracy in Reach

Focusing in advanced publicizing includes fitting efforts to explicit crowds in light of socio economics, interests, ways of behaving, and different variables. This accuracy permits promoters to convey their messages to the most pertinent people, improving the probability of commitment and changes.

Segment Focusing on: Promoters frequently start by characterizing their interest group in light of socioeconomics like age, orientation, pay, and schooling. This fundamental degree of focusing on adjusts the promotion to the attributes of the target group.

Geographic Focusing on: Geographic focusing on permits promoters to zero in their endeavors on unambiguous areas, whether it's a nation, city, or even a sweep around an actual area. This is especially helpful for organizations with restricted items or administrations.

Conduct Focusing on: Understanding client conduct is an amazing asset. Publicists can target people in light of their web-based exercises, for example, sites visited, look directed, or content drew in with. This empowers more customized and pertinent promotion conveyance.

Interest-Based Focusing on: Publicists influence information on clients' inclinations and inclinations to fit advertisements to explicit side interests, exercises, or themes. This guarantees that the substance lines up with what clients see as engaging.

Logical Focusing on: Putting promotions in settings that match the substance of the website page or application increases importance. For instance, a travel service's promotion could show up on a blog entry about colorful objections, making it bound to catch the consideration of expected explorers.

Gadget and Stage Focusing on: With the expansion of different gadgets and stages, sponsors can enhance their lobbies for explicit gadgets (work areas, PCs, cell phones, tablets) and stages (web-based entertainment, sites, applications). This guarantees a consistent client experience custom fitted to the gadget being utilized.

Fruitful focusing is a fragile equilibrium. On one hand, publicists intend to contact a wide crowd to boost perceivability; on the other, they need to guarantee their message resonates with the perfect people. Finding some kind of harmony requires a profound comprehension of the ideal interest group and consistent observing and change of focusing on boundaries.

Ad Designs: Different Ways to Get People's Attention Once you know who your target audience is, you need to choose the right ad format to make an impression that lasts. Promotion designs direct the way that the message is introduced outwardly and intuitively, affecting how clients draw in with the substance.

Show Advertisements: These are the customary standard advertisements that show up on sites and applications. Display ads can be any size and include text, images, and occasionally interactive elements. They are flexible and successful for brand mindfulness.

Video Promotions: Video ads have gained popularity as video content consumption has increased. These can be short, powerful clips that are shared on social media, websites, or streaming services and use audio and images to convey a powerful message.

Local Advertisements: Native ads offer a non-disruptive advertising experience because they blend in seamlessly with the platform's content. They match the look and feel of the encompassing substance, making them more captivating for clients.

Search Promotions: These advertisements show up at the highest point of web search tool results, regularly named as supported. They are set off by unambiguous watchwords, guaranteeing they arrive at clients effectively looking for significant data, items, or administrations.

Virtual Entertainment Promotions: Ad formats on social media platforms range from image ads to sponsored posts and carousel ads. These arrangements influence the intuitive and social nature of the stages, empowering clients to like, offer, and remark.

Intelligent Promotions: Drawing in clients with intuitive components, for example, tests, games, or surveys, can improve the general promotion experience. Intuitive advertisements advance client support, improving the probability of essential associations.

Rich Media Promotions: These promotions go past static visuals by integrating dynamic components like activities, sound, and video. Rich media promotions expect to catch consideration and make a vivid encounter, making them successful for narrating.

Picking the right promotion design relies upon the mission goals, main interest group inclinations, and the stage where the advertisements will be shown. The advantages of each format and how well they align with their overall marketing objectives must be carefully considered by advertisers.

All in all, effective computerized publicizing includes a cooperative connection between exact focusing on and significant promotion designs. Publicists should examine information, grasp their crowd, and specialty messages that reverberate. By joining the right focusing on boundaries with convincing promotion designs, advertisers can make crusades that contact the perfect individuals as well as have an enduring effect, eventually driving wanted activities and accomplishing showcasing targets.

Best Practices for Engagement

Commitment is a basic consideration of different parts of life, from individual connections to proficient conditions. Whether you are dealing with a group, maintaining a business, or developing a web-based local area, executing best practices for commitment can fundamentally upgrade your prosperity. Here, we'll investigate key techniques to cultivate significant commitment across various settings.

1. Figure out Your Crowd:

Fitting your way to deal with the particular requirements and inclinations of your crowd is principal. Whether it's clients, representatives, or online adherents, find an opportunity to figure out their socioeconomics, interests, and correspondence inclinations. This information frames the establishment for making content and encounters that impact them.

2. Clear Correspondence:

Viable correspondence is at the core of commitment. Whether it's in a meeting, a marketing campaign, or a social media post, clearly articulate your message. Use language that is available and interesting to your crowd. Avoid jargon that may cause people who are unfamiliar with industry-specific terms to become alienated.

3. Encourage Two-Way Correspondence:

Commitment is definitely not a road that goes only one direction. Facilitate and encourage open dialogue. Respond promptly, listen intently to concerns, and actively seek feedback. This two-way correspondence constructs trust and makes a feeling of local area, whether it's inside a group or between a brand and its clients.

4. Make Use of Several Channels:

Diversify your approach because people engage in a variety of ways. Consolidate a blend of face to face collaborations, messages, web-based entertainment, and other significant stages. This guarantees that you contact your crowd where they are generally agreeable and dynamic.

5. Personalization:

Tailor encounters and content to individual inclinations whenever the situation allows. Personalization causes individuals to feel seen and esteemed. Whether it's tweaking item suggestions or recognizing individual accomplishments inside a group, individual contacts upgrade the general commitment experience.

6. Set Specific Goals:

Lucidity around objectives and assumptions is urgent. Whether you're driving an undertaking or dealing with a local area, obviously characterize jobs, obligations, and goals. At the point when everybody comprehends their commitment and the general reason, it encourages a feeling of direction and responsibility.

7. Appreciation and Recognition:

Perceiving and valuing the endeavors of people develops a positive climate. Recognize accomplishments, achievements, and difficult work. Openly perceiving commitments inside a group or displaying client examples of overcoming adversity lifts the general mood as well as spurs proceeded with commitment.

8. Offer some incentive:

Whether it's through items, administrations, or content, reliably offer some benefit to your crowd. Provide solutions that improve their lives and comprehend their requirements. At the point when individuals see that drawing in with your image or group enhances their encounters, they are bound to remain involved.

9. Gamification:

Gamification can improve engagement by making it more enjoyable and rewarding. Whether it's through difficulties, rivalries, or identifications, making a feeling of rivalry or accomplishment can invigorate expanded investment.

10. Adaptability and Versatility:

Be prepared to modify your strategy in response to feedback and shifting circumstances. Flexibility demonstrates a dedication to continuous improvement and adaptability to your audience's changing requirements.

11. Energize Coordinated effort:

In group settings, cultivating coordinated effort among individuals is fundamental for commitment. Energize thought sharing, collaboration, and aggregate critical thinking. At the point when people feel their commitments are esteemed inside a cooperative climate, commitment normally thrives.

12. Accessibility:

Guarantee that your commitment endeavors are available to everybody. This includes taking into account various communication styles, preferred languages, and any potential obstacles to participation. Establishing a comprehensive climate encourages a more extensive and more practical commitment.

Taking everything into account, best practices for commitment rotate around figuring out your crowd, compelling correspondence, and making esteem. By executing these procedures, whether in an expert or individual setting, you can major areas of strength for fabrication, encourage joint effort, and establish a positive and connecting climate for all interested parties.

INSTAGRAM
Advertising

Instagram advertising is now a major force in digital marketing because it gives businesses a visually appealing way to connect with their target audience. With more than a billion month to month dynamic clients, Instagram gives an immense and different crowd that advertisers can take advantage of to advance their items or administrations.

One of the critical qualities of Instagram promoting lies in its visual-driven nature. The stage is essentially centered around pictures and recordings, permitting brands to feature their contributions in a convincing and tastefully satisfying way. This accentuation on visual substance sets aside it an ideal room for organizations in businesses like style, magnificence, travel, and food, where the visual allure is urgent for shopper commitment.

The promotion designs on Instagram are assorted, taking special care of different showcasing targets. Photograph promotions permit organizations to recount their story through a solitary, striking picture. Video advertisements, with their vivid and dynamic nature, give a chance to more expanded narrating and brand building. Merry-go -round promotions empower organizations to exhibit numerous pictures or recordings in a solitary post, empowering clients to swipe through and investigate various features of an item or administration.

Instagram Stories have arisen as an especially successful promoting design. With north of 500 million day to day dynamic clients, Stories offer a full-screen, vivid experience that enthralls the crowd's consideration. Organizations can utilize this configuration to make a story, share in the background content, or feature restricted time offers. The intuitive components inside Stories, for example, surveys and swipe-up joins, improve client commitment and drive direct activities.

Instagram's robust targeting capabilities enable advertisers to target specific demographics, interests, and behaviors. Organizations can tailor their promotions to show up in the feeds of clients who are probably going to be keen on their items, subsequently expanding the effect of their missions. Not only does this precise targeting make advertisements more relevant, but it also boosts advertisers' overall return on investment.

Instagram's integration with Facebook's advertising platform boosts its efficiency even further. Sponsors can use the broad information accessible on Facebook to make exceptionally designated Instagram crusades. The consistent association between the two stages empowers organizations to run facilitated crusades, arriving at clients across both web-based entertainment monsters and guaranteeing a far reaching web presence.

The ascent of powerhouse promoting has added one more aspect to Instagram publicizing. Brands can team up with powerhouses who have a huge following on the stage to really advance their items. Powerhouses carry an individual touch to the advancement, making it more interesting to their devotees. This type of promotion gains by the trust that powerhouses have worked with their crowd, improving the validity and effect of the brand message. The Investigate tab on Instagram gives one more road to publicizing. As clients investigate content past their nearby organization, organizations can put advertisements in this arranged disclosure space. This permits brands to interface with clients who may not follow them however share comparable interests, expanding the compass of their missions.

Instagram's shopping highlights have changed the stage into a powerful web based business objective. Organizations can label items in their posts, permitting clients to investigate and buy things flawlessly inside the application. This immediate mix of shopping into the client experience smoothes out the way from revelation to change, making Instagram an integral asset for driving deals.

Investigation and bits of knowledge are vital parts of any effective publicizing methodology, and Instagram gives a thorough set-up of devices for following execution. Promoters can screen key measurements like reach, commitment, and change, acquiring important bits of knowledge into the adequacy of their missions. This information driven approach empowers organizations to refine their procedures, upgrade promotion content, and apportion financial plans all the more really.

Be that as it may, similar to any promoting stage, Instagram isn't without its difficulties. The visual idea of the stage implies that making superior grade, outwardly engaging substance is fundamental for hanging out in a packed feed. Also, there is a lot of competition for users' attention, so businesses have to constantly come up with new ways to get people's attention and keep them interested.

Instagram advertising has emerged as a fundamental component of digital marketing due to its visually appealing platform, extensive targeting options, and variety of ad formats. The platform's strengths can be used by businesses to create compelling campaigns, connect with their target audience, and achieve measurable outcomes. As Instagram proceeds to develop and present new elements, publicists should remain spry and imaginative to take advantage of this dynamic and powerful publicizing channel.

Visual Content Strategies

In today's digital environment, where information overload is a constant challenge, visual content strategies are crucial. In a world dominated by social media, websites, and other digital platforms, it is essential to be able to effectively convey messages and attract attention. This is where visual substance methodologies become possibly the most important factor, filling in as an amazing asset for correspondence, commitment, and brand building.

Understanding who your intended audience is is the most important aspect of any successful visual content strategy. Various socio economics have differing inclinations and ways of behaving, so fitting visual substance to resonate with the target group is vital. This includes intensive investigation into the socioeconomics, interests, and online ways of behaving of the main interest group, giving significant bits of knowledge that educate the creation regarding outwardly engaging and applicable substance.

One of the most common types of visual substance is pictures. In a general public where capacities to focus are lessening, a charming picture can pass on a message more effectively than sections of message. Superior grade, stylishly satisfying pictures stand out as well as add to a positive impression of the brand. Brands put resources into proficient photography or visual communication to guarantee their visual substance sticks out and lines up with their general picture.

Additionally, the ascent of video content has reformed visual methodologies. Recordings have the ability to recount a story, feature items, and make profound associations with the crowd. Stages like YouTube, TikTok, and Instagram have become jungle gyms for video content, and organizations are utilizing these channels to draw in clients. From instructional exercise recordings to in the background sees, the flexibility of video content permits brands to associate with their crowd on a more private level.

Consistency is one more vital part of visual substance methodologies. Laying out a strong visual character across different stages helps in memorability. This incorporates utilizing predictable varieties, text styles, and plan components. Whether it's an online entertainment post, a blog realistic, or an email bulletin, keeping a brought together visual language supports the brand's character and constructs entrust with the crowd after some time.

Infographics are a common format for visual content on social media. These outwardly engaging portrayals of data are exceptionally shareable and absorbable. Infographics gather complex information into effectively reasonable visuals, making them a significant device for instructive substance. Online entertainment clients value compact, educational designs that can be immediately consumed and shared, adding to the virality of content.

User-generated content (UGC) integration is yet another successful strategy. A genuine connection is established between a brand and its target audience when customers are encouraged to share their product or service-related experiences. UGC fills in as friendly verification, displaying genuine individuals profiting from the brand. Sharing this content cultivates a feeling of local area as well as gives free advancement, as fulfilled clients become brand advocates.

In the time of cell phones, advancing visual substance for portable utilization is non-debatable. With most web clients getting to content on cell phones, visuals should be effectively distinguishable on more modest screens. This includes utilizing responsive plan, high-goal pictures, and succinct subtitles to guarantee a consistent client experience across gadgets.

Virtual entertainment stages offer various highlights for visual narrating. Instagram, for example, permits brands to organize an outwardly engaging feed using lattices and merry go rounds. Stories and reels open doors to additional dynamic and intuitive substance. Utilizing these elements upgrades a brand's capacity to interface with the crowd in different ways, keeping content new and locking in.

Also, integrating visual inquiry into the system is building up some decent forward movement. Visual pursuit permits clients to look for items or data utilizing pictures instead of text. This innovation opens up additional opportunities for web based business, empowering clients to find items they will be unable to depict precisely. As visual inquiry capacities develop, brands that streamline their visual substance for this pattern stand to acquire an upper hand.

All in all, visual substance procedures are necessary to successful correspondence in the advanced age. Whether through pictures, recordings, infographics, or client created content, brands should use visuals to catch consideration, pass on messages, and assemble enduring associations with their crowd. Figuring out the objective segment, keeping up with consistency, and adjusting to developing patterns, for example, visual inquiry are fundamental parts of an effective visual substance methodology. As the computerized scene keeps on developing, marks that focus on and advance in their visual substance procedures will flourish in catching and holding the consideration of their crowd.

Influencer Collaborations

As of late, powerhouse coordinated efforts have turned into a strong showcasing procedure, forming the scene of computerized promoting and purchaser commitment. Beyond conventional advertising strategies, the synergy between brands and influencers has resulted in a dynamic and mutually beneficial relationship.

At its center, a powerhouse joint effort includes a brand cooperating with an online entertainment powerhouse to advance its items or administrations. This partnership makes use of the influencer's established credibility, authenticity, and reach within a particular niche or audience. The force to be reckoned with, thus, accesses new open doors, extended perceivability, and likely monetary impetuses.

One of the vital benefits of powerhouse coordinated efforts is the capacity to take advantage of a devoted and connected crowd. Powerhouses have developed a local area around their substance, encouraging a feeling of trust and association with their supporters. At the point when a brand conforms to a powerhouse whose qualities and feel resound with its objective segment, it can use the powerhouse's validity to fabricate trust and realness.

Besides, powerhouse coordinated efforts give marks a road to arrive at more youthful and more tricky socioeconomics. As conventional publicizing channels battle to catch the consideration of Age Z and twenty to thirty year olds, forces to be reckoned with act as an extension among brands and these sought after buyer gatherings. The appeal of powerhouses, who frequently share individual stories, encounters, and inclinations, makes a more bona fide association with more youthful crowds.

The progress of powerhouse coordinated efforts isn't exclusively founded on the force to be reckoned with adherent count yet in addition on the arrangement of values and the making of drawing is satisfied. Realness is principal in force to be reckoned with. Shoppers are progressively knowing and can undoubtedly recognize inauthentic advancements. Thus, brands should cautiously choose powerhouses whose content flawlessly coordinates their items or administrations into the force to be reckoned with laid out story.

Notwithstanding realness, imagination assumes a crucial part in the viability of powerhouse joint efforts. Fruitful organizations include something beyond an item situation; they involve the co-production of a convincing substance that resonates with the powerhouse's crowd. This cooperative substance frequently appears as supported posts, item surveys, unpacking recordings, or even restricted release stock planned related to the force to be reckoned with.

Past the computerized domain, powerhouse joint efforts have gushed out into the actual world, with powerhouses wandering into item dispatches and selective occasions. This assembly of on the web and disconnected encounters further reinforces the connection between the powerhouse, the brand, and the crowd. Participants at powerhouse facilitated occasions, for instance, draw in with the force to be reckoned with straightforwardly as well as become piece of a common encounter, extending their association with the brand.

Notwithstanding the various advantages, powerhouse coordinated efforts accompany their own arrangement of difficulties. The scene is immersed, and picking the right powerhouse requires conscious thought. Brands should lead intensive exploration to guarantee that a powerhouse's qualities line up with theirs and that their crowd truly draws in with the substance.

Additionally, there is an inborn gamble related to powerhouse advertising, as powerhouses are people with their own viewpoints, convictions, and ways of behaving. Debates encompassing powerhouses have featured the possible entanglements of these associations, underlining the significance of a reasonable level of effort in the determination cycle. Brands need to evaluate a force to be reckoned with compass as well as their standing and the possible effect of any past discussions.

As the powerhouse showcasing scene develops, so do the measurements for estimating achievement. Past the conventional measurements of reach and commitment, brands are progressively centered around measurements that exhibit unmistakable business influence, for example, change rates, deals attribution, and profit from venture. Forces to be reckoned with are currently expected to give something other than perceivability; they are essential to the whole client venture, from attention to change.

All in all, force to be reckoned with coordinated efforts have changed the showcasing scene by tackling the force of special interactions and true narrating. When executed insightfully, these organizations can raise a brand's perceivability, connect with explicit socioeconomics, and cultivate a feeling of locality. As the computerized space keeps on developing, powerhouse coordinated efforts are probably going to stay a vital procedure for brands expecting to explore the constantly changing scene of customer commitment.

LINKEDIN Advertising

LinkedIn publicizing is a useful asset for organizations hoping to interface with experts, fabricate brand mindfulness, and produce leads in the B2B space. With more than 700 million clients around the world, LinkedIn gives an interesting stage to focusing on unambiguous socioeconomics in light of expert capabilities, making it a priceless asset for organizations expecting to arrive at leaders.

One of the vital qualities of LinkedIn promoting is its capacity to focus on a profoundly unambiguous crowd. Promoters can tailor their missions in view of different rules, for example, work title, organization size, industry, and, surprisingly, explicit LinkedIn gatherings. This granularity guarantees that your promotions arrive at the right experts, improving the probability of commitment and changes.

Supported Content is one of the most well-known promotion designs on LinkedIn, showing up straightforwardly in clients' feeds. These local promotions mix consistently with natural substance, offering a non-problematic client experience. Publicists can utilize Supported Content to advance blog entries, contextual analyses, or other important substance, cultivating commitment and trust among their main interest group.

LinkedIn's Supported InMail is another compelling publicizing choice. Advertisers can now send personalized messages directly to LinkedIn users' inboxes thanks to this feature. For targeted campaigns, such as promoting webinars, events, or exclusive offers, this direct approach can have a significant impact. Nonetheless, it's urgent to make convincing messages to try not to be seen as spam.

For organizations zeroed in on lead age, LinkedIn's Lead Gen Structures work on the cycle. With just a few clicks, these pre-filled forms collect user information and are displayed directly within the advertisement. By limiting the means expected for clients to communicate interest, Lead Gen Structures improve the probability of transformations. It's an important instrument for organizations hoping to develop their client base or support possible clients.

The stage's vigorous investigation furnished publicists with savvy information on crusade execution. From impressions and snaps to segment data about the crowd, LinkedIn's examination assists promoters with refining their systems. This information driven approach permits organizations to upgrade their missions continuously, guaranteeing that their promoting financial plan is distributed really.

LinkedIn additionally offers dynamic promoting arrangements, like Merry go round Advertisements. This configuration permits promoters to exhibit numerous pictures or recordings inside a solitary promotion, giving an outwardly captivating method for recounting a brand's story or feature various items. Carousel Ads' interactive nature can pique users' interest and encourage them to learn more about the brand.

One of the new increments to LinkedIn's promoting arms stockpile is Discussion Advertisements. Direct prospect interaction is made possible by these interactive message-based ads. Sponsors can utilize Discussion Promotions to make a customized visit like insight, directing clients through a progression of inquiries or data. Businesses are able to gain a deeper understanding of their target market thanks to this format's emphasis on meaningful interaction.

LinkedIn's retargeting choices further upgrade the adequacy of missions. By retargeting clients who have collaborated with past promotions or visited a particular presentation page, sponsors can remain top-of-brain and reconnect likely leads. This guarantees that promoting endeavors are centered around the individuals who have proactively shown interest, expanding the possibilities of transformation.

To take full advantage of LinkedIn publicizing, organizations ought to streamline their organization profiles. A convincing and proficient profile builds trust and believability among clients who experience supported content. Moreover, adjusting the promotion duplicate and visuals to the general brand picture is critical for making a strong and important experience.

It's essential to take note of that while LinkedIn publicizing offers various benefits, it likewise requires cautious preparation and progressing enhancement. A successful LinkedIn advertising strategy necessitates regular campaign performance analysis, modification of targeting criteria, and refinement of ad creatives.

All in all, LinkedIn promoting is a strong device for organizations looking to interface with experts and leaders in the B2B space. With an assortment of promotion designs, focusing on choices, and hearty examination, sponsors can tailor their lobbies for most extreme effect. By utilizing the stage's extraordinary elements, organizations can assemble brand mindfulness, produce leads, and lay out significant associations inside their main interest group.

Professional Audience Targeting

Proficient crowd focusing is a basic part of any effective promoting system. In the present cutthroat business scene, arriving at the right experts with your message can have the effect between a mission's prosperity and disappointment. This interaction includes distinguishing, fragmenting, and connecting with explicit expert gatherings to augment the effect of promoting endeavors.

Understanding the characteristics and actions of the target audience is an essential component of professional audience targeting. To learn about the demographics, interests, and preferences of the professionals you want to reach, thorough research is required. By social occasion information on variables, for example, work titles, ventures, and geological areas, advertisers can make point by point profiles that guide their effort endeavors. The coming of computerized innovations has upset the manner in which experts consume data. Online stages, virtual entertainment, and expert organizations assume an urgent part in coming to and drawing in proficient crowds. Virtual entertainment stages like LinkedIn, for example, give an abundance of focusing on choices, permitting advertisers to tailor their messages in view of occupation titles, organization size, and other significant rules.

Making customized and applicable substances is one more key part of the expert crowd focusing on. Experts are bound to draw in with content that tends to their particular requirements, difficulties, and interests. Thus, advertisers ought to create content that talks straightforwardly to the trouble spots of their ideal interest group, offering important experiences and arrangements. This might incorporate whitepapers, contextual analyses, online classes, and different arrangements that reverberate with experts in the designated business.

Email showcasing stays an incredible asset for contacting proficient crowds. However, the capacity to deliver content that is both personalized and pertinent is essential to the success of email campaigns. Advertisers can use information to portion their email records and send designated messages to explicit expert gatherings. Personalization, for example, tending to beneficiaries by their names and fitting substance in view of their inclinations, improves the adequacy of email advertising in a proficient crowd focusing on.

Events and conferences offer valuable opportunities to connect with professional audiences in addition to digital channels. Supporting or taking part in industry-explicit occasions permits advertisers to connect straightforwardly with experts in a more private setting. This up close and personal association can fabricate trust and believability, making it almost certain that experts will recall and draw in with the brand.

Furthermore, professional audience targeting strategies can only be refined and improved through the use of data analytics. It is beneficial to examine campaign performance metrics like click-through rates, conversion rates, and engagement levels to learn what works and what needs to be improved. By ceaselessly observing and changing focusing on boundaries in light of execution information, advertisers can improve the accuracy and viability of their missions.

Moral contemplations likewise assume a critical part in a proficient crowd focusing on. Any marketing strategy must take into account the importance of protecting customer data and privacy. Advertisers should guarantee that the strategies used to gather and use information are straightforward and conform to important regulations. Building trust with the expert crowd is fundamental, and straightforward correspondence about information utilization rehearses encourages a positive connection between the brand and its main interest group.

Effective expert crowd focusing requires a dynamic and versatile methodology. The expert scene advances, thus do the inclinations and ways of behaving of the main interest group. Advertisers should remain informed about industry patterns, mechanical headways, and work on proficient propensities to likewise change their methodologies.

In conclusion, professional audience targeting is a multifaceted procedure that requires in-depth investigation, individualized content creation, and the strategic utilization of various channels. The capacity to comprehend and associate with the particular necessities and interests of expert crowds is a vital differentiator in the serious business climate. By utilizing a thorough and information driven approach, advertisers can really reach, draw in, and construct enduring associations with their objective expert fragments.

Content Optimization for B2B

Content streamlining for B2B (Business-to-Business) is a basic part of computerized promoting techniques, pointed toward upgrading the perceivability, significance, and effect of content custom fitted for organizations. Effective content optimization has the potential to significantly influence the buyer's journey and contribute to successful conversions in a market where businesses engage in complex decision-making processes. In order to meet the changing requirements of B2B audiences, this comprehensive strategy incorporates keyword research, strategic planning, and constant refinement.

One vital component of content advancement for B2B is figuring out the interest group. In contrast to B2C (Business-to-Consumer), B2B transactions frequently involve multiple internal decision-makers. Accordingly, satisfied ought to address the worries, difficulties, and desires of different partners, going from leaders to powerhouses and end-clients. Creating purchaser personas that include the jobs and obligations of these people is critical for fitting substance that resounds with the whole dynamic unit.

Key watchword research is one more foundation of B2B content enhancement. Recognizing and focusing on pertinent watchwords that line up with the business, business goals, and problem areas of the interest group is fundamental for site improvement (Website optimization). Long-tail catchphrases, well defined for the B2B space, can be especially successful in catching the consideration of specialty crowds and situating the substance as a significant asset in the business.

Consistency across diverts is fundamental in B2B content streamlining. Whether it's the organization site, blog entries, online entertainment, or email crusades, keeping a bound together brand voice and informing guarantees a firm and noteworthy experience for the crowd. The brand's authority in the market is also bolstered by this consistency, which builds trust.

Utilizing information examination devices is essential to effective substance streamlining in the B2B domain. These apparatuses give experiences into client conduct, commitment measurements, and the exhibition of various bits of content. Marketers can refine content strategies, prioritize topics that drive the most value for the business, and make informed decisions about what resonates with the audience by analyzing this data.

Personalization is a major trend in B2B content optimization. Relevance and engagement are increased by tailoring content to specific industries, company sizes, and roles within organizations. This can be accomplished through unique substance, customized proposals, and designated informing in light of the client's situation in the deals pipe. The more customized the substance, the almost certain it is to catch the consideration of leaders and forces to be reckoned with.

Consolidating sight and sound components is one more viable methodology in B2B content advancement. Infographics, videos, and interactive presentations are examples of visual content that can effectively and more effectively convey complex information. This not only makes the user experience better but also takes into account the various learning styles of the B2B audience.

Advancing substance for cell phones is fundamental in the cutting edge B2B scene. Leaders frequently access data in a hurry, and versatile substance guarantees openness and a consistent encounter across different gadgets. Responsive plan, quick stacking times, and brief yet significant substance are urgent contemplations for versatile enhancement in the B2B setting.

The developing idea of B2B ventures requires a pledge to ceaseless improvement. Consistently reviewing and refreshing existing substance keeps it pertinent and adjusts it to industry patterns and changes. This proactive methodology keeps up with the intensity of the substance as well as shows a pledge to give state-of-the-art and important data to the interest group.

All in all, happy enhancement for B2B includes a diverse methodology that considers the exceptional qualities of the ideal interest group, key utilization of watchwords, consistency across channels, information driven direction, personalization, sight and sound mix, versatile streamlining, and a pledge to ceaseless improvement. By embracing these standards, organizations can situate themselves as definitive assets inside their enterprises, really draw in leaders, and drive fruitful B2B changes.

Chapter 2 Crafting Compelling Content and Visual Design Tips

Making convincing substance and carrying out powerful visual plans are urgent components for making an effective and connected computerized presence. Whether you are planning a site, making virtual entertainment posts, or creating showcasing materials, the cooperative energy among content and visual plan can fundamentally influence the client experience and generally speaking viability of your message.

The Force of Convincing Substance
Content is the foundation of any correspondence technique. Creating a convincing substance includes something other than passing on data; it requires figuring out your crowd, conveying a reasonable message, and getting a close to home reaction. Here are key contemplations for making content that dazzles:

Comprehend where Your Audience members may come from:
Know your target audience's demographics, preferences, and requirements.
Create content that speaks to the values and interests of your audience.

Clearness and Compactness:
Convey your message in an unmistakable and succinct way.
Utilize straightforward language and construct your
substance legitimately to improve lucidness.

Storytelling:
Weave a story that draws in your crowd inwardly.
To make your content more memorable, share
stories or case studies that people can relate to.

Offer:
Obviously convey the worth your item, administration, or data brings.
Feature advantages and answers for the crowd's trouble spots.

Visual Allure in Text:
Separate enormous pieces of text with subheadings, list items, and visuals.
Pick textual styles and organizing that improve lucidness.

Visual Plan Tips for Effective Show

Visual plan supplements convincing substance by making an outwardly engaging and firm insight. Here are fundamental ways to upgrade the visual part of your correspondence:

Reliable Marking:

Keep a steady visual character across all stages.

Utilize a strong variety range, text styles, and logo to support memorability.

Whitespace Usage:

Embrace whitespace to forestall visual mess.

Satisfactory separating further develops clarity and focuses on key components.

Pictures and Designs:

Integrate excellent pictures and illustrations pertinent to your substance.

Enhance visuals for speedy stacking, guaranteeing a consistent client experience.

Typography Matters:

Pick textual styles that line up with your image and are not difficult to peruse.

Make strategic use of font sizes and styles to emphasize crucial information.

Order and Stream:

Lay out a visual order to direct the watcher's eye.

Establish a logical flow for the content and guide the audience through it.

Responsive Plan:

Guarantee your plan adjusts to various gadgets and screen sizes.

Responsive plan is critical for a predictable client experience across stages.

Intelligent Components:

Consolidate intelligent components like buttons, movements, or recordings.

Engaging the user and keeping their attention can be enhanced by interactive features.

Accessibility:
Focus on availability by giving elective text to pictures and guaranteeing variety contrast.

A plan that considers openness takes special care of a more extensive crowd.

Accomplishing Agreement among Content and Plan

Coordinated effort is Critical:
Encourage joint effort between satisfied makers and fashioners.

Guarantee a bound together vision that adjusts both the composed and visual viewpoints.

Prototyping and wireframing:
Make wireframes or models to imagine the format and cooperation.

The finished product can be improved through iterative collaboration using prototypes.

Client Testing:
Assemble input through client testing to refine both substance and plan.

Comprehend client inclinations and make changes likewise.

Adaptability:
Be available to adjust content and configuration in light of client criticism and evolving patterns.

Adaptability considers nonstop improvement and significance.

Information Driven Advancement:
Examine information on client conduct, commitment, and transformations.

Utilize insights to improve performance by optimizing content and design.

Mobile-First Strategy:
Focus on versatile responsiveness in plan and content format.

Numerous clients access content on cell phones, and a versatile plan is basic.

a memorable and powerful digital experience is only possible if compelling content and effective visual design work together. Figuring out your crowd, creating a convincing story, and executing smart visual plan components all in all add to the progress of your correspondence endeavors. By consistently refining both substance and configuration in view of client criticism and information bits of knowledge, you can guarantee a dynamic and drawing in web-based presence that resounds with your crowd.

Copywriting Techniques

Copywriting is a flexible and fundamental expertise in the domain of showcasing and promoting, impacting how items and administrations are seen by possible clients. Effective copywriting goes past simple words; it includes an essential mix of imagination, brain science, and market getting it. In this investigation of copywriting methods, we'll dig into key rules that can lift your composition and assist you with associating with your ideal interest group.

One key part of powerful copywriting is figuring out the interest group. It is essential to know who you are speaking to before you write a single word. What are their requirements, wants, and trouble spots? Leading exhaustive statistical surveying and making purchaser personas can give significant bits of knowledge. Fitting your message to reverberate with your crowd lays out an association, making them bound to draw in with your substance.

Storytelling is yet another effective strategy. People are intrinsically attracted to accounts, and consolidating narrating into your duplicate can make it more appealing and critical. Rather than barraging your crowd with highlights and insights, recount to a convincing story that exhibits the advantages and genuine uses of your item or administration. This profound association can essentially influence shopper discernment and direction.

The significance of a convincing title couldn't possibly be more significant. A catchy headline is the first step toward engaging your audience in the digital age, when attention spans are short. Whether it's offering an interesting conversation starter, promising an answer, or making interest, a very much created title captivates users to dig further into your duplicate. Set aside some margin to try different things with various title styles to find what reverberates best with your crowd.

Whenever you've caught consideration with a solid title, keeping up with interest all through the duplicate is pivotal. Utilize compact and connecting with language, zeroing in on benefits as opposed to simply includes. What a product or service can do for a customer is more important to them than its technical specifications. Featuring the worth and special selling suggestions keeps perusers intrigued and puts resources into your message.

The influential ability is a foundation of viable copywriting. Use mental triggers to impact independent direction. Including elements like scarcity, authority, and social proof can instill a sense of urgency and credibility. Restricted time offers, tributes, and supports from perceived figures can influence customer conduct and upgrade the enticing effect of your duplicate.

While influence is fundamental, straightforwardness assembles trust. Speak the truth about your item or administration, and keep away from poetic overstatement that might prompt frustration. Modern consumers, who are becoming more discerning regarding marketing strategies, respond well to authenticity. Make sure your copy matches the actual customer experience and clearly communicate what your offering can offer.

The design of your duplicate is basically as significant as the actual substance. Separate your message into effectively absorbable areas with clear headings and subheadings. Use list items and brief sections to upgrade lucidness. A well-organized structure ensures that your key points are easily accessible in the digital environment, where users frequently skim content.

Underscoring the advantages of your contribution is more compelling than posting highlights. Customers need to know how an item or administration will work in their lives. Concentrate on addressing problems and offering solutions. Whether it's saving time, improving prosperity, or taking care of a particular issue, obviously impart the positive effect your contribution can have on the client.

A convincing source of inspiration (CTA) is the key part of successful copywriting. Obviously teach your crowd on the ideal subsequent stage, whether it's making a buy, pursuing a bulletin, or mentioning more data. Utilize powerful language in your CTA, stressing the advantages of making a move. Try different things with various states and situations to improve the adequacy of your source of inspiration.

All in all, excelling at copywriting includes a diverse methodology that joins figuring out your crowd, narrating, convincing strategies, straightforwardness, and successful organizing. By integrating these procedures into your composition, you can make convincing duplicates that catches consideration as well as drives activity. Continue refining and exploring different avenues regarding your way to deal with finding what reverberates best with your interest group, and recall that fruitful copywriting is a continuous course of transformation and improvement.

Video Advertising Insights

Video publicizing has turned into a vital device in the advanced promoting scene, offering brands a vivid and connecting method for associating with their main interest group. As innovation keeps on propelling, video promotions develop, introducing new difficulties and valuable open doors for advertisers. We delve into key trends, strategies, and the impact on consumer behavior in this investigation of video advertising insights.

The rise of short-form videos is one prominent video advertising trend. Stages like TikTok and Instagram Reels have promoted snackable substances, provoking sponsors to reexamine their methodology. With abilities to focus waning, compact and charming recordings have shown to be more compelling. Advertisers are presently utilizing these stages to make noteworthy, scaled down commercials that rapidly catch the watcher's consideration.

Personalization has likewise arisen as a basic figure video promoting achievement. With information examination and computerized reasoning, publicists can tailor content in light of client inclinations, socioeconomics, and online way of behaving. Customized video advertisements improve the watcher experience as well as improve the probability of transformation. This move toward content that is hyper-targeted shows how important it is to know your audience and send messages that resonate with each person.

Besides, intuitive video advertisements are building up forward movement. Watchers are as of now not detached buyers; they look for vivid encounters. Intuitive recordings permit clients to

53

draw in with the substance, pursuing decisions that influence the account or investigate extra data. This two-way correspondence upgrades brand-buyer connections and makes a more important brand insight.

The combination of shoppable video promotions addresses a consistent intermingling of online business and video publicizing. Stages like YouTube and Instagram currently permit clients to buy items straightforwardly from the video, wiping out grinding in the client venture. Advertisers benefit from a measurable return on investment as a result of this direct link between discovery and purchase.

While the previously mentioned patterns feature the dynamism of video promoting, the significance of narrating stays consistent. A convincing story has the ability to bring out feelings and fabricate an association with the crowd. Brands that effectively mesh narrating into their video promotions can have an enduring effect, cultivating brand unwaveringly and support.

Video promotion via online entertainment stages has turned into a foundation of many showcasing procedures. The sheer volume of clients on stages like Facebook, Instagram, and Twitter makes them ideal spaces for contacting assorted crowds. Publicists influence the focusing on abilities of these stages to guarantee their video content contacts the perfect individuals, brilliantly, and in the right setting.

In any case, the rising pervasiveness of promotion obstructing programming represents a test to video publicists. As buyers become more proficient at keeping away from customary promoting, brands should track down inventive ways of catching consideration. This has prompted the investigation of local promoting inside video content, where brands consistently coordinate their message into the client experience, staying away from the meddlesome idea of conventional advertisements.

Measurements assume a critical part in assessing the progress of video publicizing efforts. Past view counts, measurements like commitment rate, active clicking factor, and change rate give important bits of knowledge into the viability of the substance. Breaking down these measurements empowers sponsors to refine their methodologies, streamline focusing on, and allot assets all the more effectively.

The worldwide shift to versatile utilization has additionally reshaped video promoting methodologies. As cell phones become the essential gadget for content utilization, vertical and square video designs have acquired conspicuousness. Adjusting to these organizations guarantees that the substance is streamlined for versatile review, boosting its effect and commitment.

All in all, video promoting keeps on developing, driven by mechanical headways and changes in purchaser conduct. Short-structure recordings, personalization, intelligence, shoppable advertisements, and narrating are characterizing the ongoing scene. Web-based entertainment stages stay key channels for contacting crowds, yet the test lies in beating promotion obstructing and conveying content that dazzles in the midst of an ocean of computerized commotion. A dynamic strategy that takes into account innovation, analytics, and a thorough comprehension of the target audience is essential to the success of video advertising. Marketers must adapt their video advertising strategies continuously to stay ahead of the curve as the digital landscape changes.

Chapter 3
Analytics and Measurement

Dissecting and estimating the effect of online entertainment publicizing is urgent for organizations looking to advance their computerized promoting systems. In the steadily advancing scene of web-based entertainment stages, understanding the adequacy of missions is fundamental for settling on informed choices and boosting profit from speculation (return for capital invested). This includes an extensive way to deal with investigation and estimation, incorporating different measurements, instruments, and strategies.

1. Key Measurements:
One of the essential parts of virtual entertainment promoting investigation is distinguishing and following key measurements. A campaign's performance is fundamentally measured

by impressions, clicks, engagement rates, and conversions. Impressions measure the times a promotion is shown, while clicks give understanding into client interest. Commitment rates, determined by associations (likes, remarks, shares) separated by impressions, measure the crowd's reaction. Transformations, addressing wanted activities like buys or recruits, straightforwardly associate with the mission's prosperity.

2. Analytics Specific to a Platform:

Different web-based entertainment stages offer novel examination instruments customized to their particular highlights. For example, Facebook Experiences gives a point by point outline of page and promotion execution, including socioeconomics, reach, and commitment measurements. Instagram Insights focuses on metrics like likes, comments, and story views for visual content. Using stage explicit investigation guarantees a designated evaluation of mission viability in light of the subtleties of every web-based entertainment channel.

3. Attribution Demonstrating:

A sophisticated method for comprehending the customer journey from initial interaction to conversion is attributed modeling. It includes allotting worth to various touchpoints in the advertising pipe, assisting organizations with distinguishing which channels and advertisements contribute most to changes. Normal attribution models incorporate first-click, last-click, and multi-contact, each offering an unmistakable viewpoint on the client's dynamic interaction. A strong attribution model is fundamental for streamlining promotion spend and refining focusing on systems.

4. Social Tuning in:

Past conventional measurements, social listening apparatuses permit organizations to screen discussions and feelings encompassing their image or industry. Following notices, feeling examination, and moving subjects give important experiences into the crowd's insight. Social listening not just guides in that frame of mind by recognizing potential issues from the beginning yet in addition guides future substance creation in light of crowd interests and inclinations.

5. The A/B Test:

A/B testing includes making varieties of a promotion and estimating their exhibition against one another. This technique recognizes the best components, whether it's the promotion duplicate, visuals, or focusing on boundaries. By methodically testing various factors, organizations can refine their web-based entertainment publicizing methodologies, further developing generally crusade adequacy.

6. Return on Promotion Spend (ROAS):

A crucial metric known as ROAS measures how much money is made for every dollar spent on advertising. Determined by isolating the income created by the promotion crusade by the expense of the mission, ROAS gives an unmistakable image of the mission's productivity. A positive ROAS demonstrates a beneficial mission, while a negative value recommends that changes are expected to further develop execution.

7. Client Lifetime Worth (CLV):

When evaluating the impact of campaigns as a whole, it is essential to comprehend the customer's long-term value acquired through social media advertising. CLV considers the income a client is supposed to create over their whole relationship with a business. By considering CLV, organizations can settle on additional educated conclusions about the amount to put resources into obtaining new clients and holding existing ones.

8. Compliance and Data Privacy:

In the period of expanding worry over information security, organizations should focus on consistence with guidelines like GDPR and CCPA. Guaranteeing that information assortment and examination rehearses comply with these guidelines safeguards client security as well as protections organizations from expected lawful results. Maintaining audience trust necessitates open communication about data usage and providing opt-out options.

9. Analytics in real time:

Real-time analytics make it possible for businesses to quickly respond to shifting user behavior and trends in social media. Observing continuous information empowers opportune acclimations to crusades, enhancing focusing on, spending plan assignment, and content in light of quick criticism.

10. Consistent Streamlining:

In social media advertising, analytics and measurement are not one-time activities but rather an ongoing process of improvement. Campaigns remain effective and in line with business goals if metrics are regularly reviewed, new strategies are tested, and new trends are adapted.

All in all, a hearty examination and estimation procedure is vital for web-based entertainment promoting achievement. Businesses can gain valuable insights, optimize their campaigns, and ultimately achieve a higher ROI by utilizing a combination of key metrics, platform-specific tools, attribution modeling, and advanced methods like social listening and A/B testing. With a promise to information driven independent direction and consistency with security guidelines, organizations can explore the unique scene of online entertainment promoting and interface with their ideal interest group really.

Key Metrics to Track and Performance Analysis Tools

Key metric tracking and the use of performance analysis tools have become essential to success in the ever-evolving business and technology landscape. Organizations, both enormous and little, depend on information driven bits of knowledge to pursue informed choices, improve cycles, and remain serious.

Understanding the critical measurements to follow and choosing the right exhibition examination instruments are vital parts of a powerful business.

Key Measurements to Track
Income and Net revenues:
Checking income streams and overall revenues gives an unmistakable image of the monetary wellbeing of a business. Strategic adjustments to pricing, cost structures, and the overall business strategy are made possible by tracking these metrics.

Client Securing Cost (CAC) and Client Lifetime Worth (CLV):
While CLV predicts the total revenue a company can anticipate from a customer throughout their entire relationship, CAC helps assess the cost of acquiring a new customer. Adjusting these measurements guarantees that client obtaining endeavors are practical and maintainable.

Change Rates:
Transformation rates uncover how really a business is transforming leads into clients. Examining change rates at different phases of the deals channel distinguishes bottlenecks and regions for development in the client venture.

Beat Rate:
Beat rate estimates the level of clients who quit utilizing an item or administration over a particular period. High agitate rates might demonstrate issues with consumer loyalty or item pertinence, accentuating the

requirement for maintenance procedures.

Consumer loyalty (CSAT) and Net Advertiser Score (NPS):

CSAT estimates consumer loyalty with an item or administration, while NPS checks the probability of clients prescribing the business to other people. Checking these measurements assists organizations with grasping their clients' opinions and further developing generally speaking brand insight.

Site Traffic and Change Sources:

Dissecting site traffic and understanding transformation sources (e.g., natural pursuit, paid promoting, virtual entertainment) gives bits of knowledge into the adequacy of advertising channels. This data supports upgrading showcasing spending plans and procedures.

Stock Turnover:

For organizations engaged with selling actual items, stock turnover estimates how rapidly items are sold and restocked. Finding some kind of harmony forestalls overloading or stockouts, improving income and functional proficiency.

Worker Efficiency and Fulfillment:

Worker measurements, for example, efficiency levels and occupation fulfillment, are basic for the general wellbeing of an association. Cheerful and connected workers are bound to contribute emphatically to an organization's prosperity.

Execution Investigation Instruments

Google Investigation:

Google Examination is a flexible instrument for site and application investigation. It gives significant bits of knowledge into client conduct, traffic sources, and change rates, engaging organizations to settle on information driven choices for their web-based presence.

HubSpot:
HubSpot is an across the board showcasing, deals, and administration stage. It offers highlights like CRM, promoting computerization, and investigation, empowering organizations to oversee client collaborations and track execution across different divisions.

Tableau:
Scene is a strong information perception instrument that changes crude information into justifiable and significant bits of knowledge. Businesses can use its interactive dashboards to visually explore and share data, which helps them make better decisions.

Salesforce:
Salesforce is a main client relationship at the board (CRM) stage. It helps organizations oversee and investigate client corporations, track leads, and figure deals, cultivating an all encompassing way to deal with client connections.

Hotjar:
Hotjar is a client conduct examination instrument that gives bits of knowledge into site ease of use. It offers heatmaps, meeting accounts, and overviews, permitting organizations to comprehend how clients collaborate with their sites and distinguish regions for development.

QuickBooks:
Accounting software like QuickBooks is used by many businesses to manage their finances, keep track of expenses,

and create financial reports. It works on monetary following and guarantees exactness in monetary administration.

Analytics from Adobe:

Adobe Investigation is a far reaching examination arrangement that covers web, portable, and disconnected channels. It gives continuous investigation, client division, and prescient examination, offering a strong stage for grasping client conduct.

Trello:

Trello is an undertaking the board instrument that works with coordinated effort and errand following. While not zeroed in on examination, it helps groups sort out and focus on assignments, upgrading by and large efficiency and undertaking the executives.

Taking everything into account, following key measurements and using execution investigation devices are crucial parts of present day business for the executives. By consistently observing key execution pointers and utilizing the right instruments, organizations can adjust to advertise changes, improve tasks, and remain in front of the opposition. The cooperative energy between shrewd measurements and compelling instruments frames the foundation of a fruitful, information driven business system.

Chapter 4
Budgeting and ROI

Any effective social media advertising strategy relies heavily on budgeting and return on investment (ROI). In the steadily developing computerized scene, organizations should apportion assets really to augment their compass and commitment. We should dive into the complexities of planning for virtual entertainment promotion and how return on initial capital investment assumes an urgent part in deciding the outcome of these missions.

Budgeting for Advertising on Social Media:

Deciding the right spending plan for web-based entertainment publicizing requires an essential methodology. It involves looking at things like the goals of the business, the people you want to reach, and the platforms you use. Every virtual entertainment stage offers different publicizing choices, and understanding the subtleties of each is urgent.

Set Clear Goals:

Start by characterizing explicit and quantifiable targets. Whether it's rising image mindfulness, driving site traffic, or helping deals, having clear objectives will direct your spending plan designation.

Understand Your Listeners' perspective:

Understanding your ideal interest group is fundamental. Various socioeconomics draw in with virtual entertainment in unmistakable ways. Tailor your financial plan to successfully contact the right crowd.

Stage Choice:

Pick the stages that line up with your crowd and targets. Each social media platform—Facebook, Instagram, Twitter, LinkedIn, and TikTok—has its own distinct user bases and advertising capabilities. Apportion financial plan in light of the stages probably going to yield the ideal outcomes.

Promotion Arrangement and Innovative:

The sort of promotion and its imaginative components influence costs. Interactive content may necessitate a larger budget, and video advertisements typically cost more than static images. To get the most out of your audience's engagement, put money into engaging content.

Testing and Streamlining:

A portion of your budget should be allocated to testing and optimization. Run A/B tests to recognize the best promotion varieties. Constantly refine your system in light of execution information to accomplish improved results over the long run.

Thought of Irregularity:

Consider any irregularity or industry-explicit patterns that might influence your mission. Change your spending plan in a manner to benefit from top periods or explore through low seasons all the more proficiently.

Observing and Changing:
Consistently screen the exhibition of your advertisements. On the off chance that specific missions or promotion sets are beating others, consider redistributing financial plans to benefit from what works best. Adaptability is key in streamlining your web-based entertainment publicizing spending plan.

Profit from Speculation (return for money invested) in Online Entertainment Promoting:
Your social media advertising efforts' profitability is measured by the ROI metric. Working out return for capital invested includes contrasting the increases from the mission with the expenses brought about. In the world of social media advertising, the following is how to approach ROI:

Characterize Measurements and Objectives:
Obviously frame the key exhibition markers (KPIs) lined up with your business objectives. Whether it's snaps, changes, or income created, laying out these measurements is fundamental for estimating return for money invested precisely.

Attribution Models:
Online entertainment promotion frequently includes various touchpoints before a transformation happens. Use attribution models to comprehend the client venture and assign worth to every cooperation. This makes it easier to give the conversion the right name.

Change Following:
Carry out powerful transformation following systems. Virtual entertainment stages give instruments to follow transformations, empowering you to

quantify the effect of your promotions on client activities, for example, buys or recruits.

CPA, or cost per acquisition, is:

Compute the expense per procurement by partitioning the complete publicizing spend by the quantity of changes. This shows how much it costs to get a new customer from your social media advertising efforts.

Lifetime Worth (LTV):

Consider the lifetime worth of a client while assessing return for money invested. Your social media advertising is generating a positive return on investment (ROI) if the customer lifetime value exceeds the cost of acquiring a customer.

Checking Web-based Entertainment Investigation:

Influence the examination given by web-based entertainment stages. These experiences help in grasping the presentation of your promotions, crowd commitment, and transformation rates. Routinely dissect these measurements to refine your procedure.

Benchmarking Against Industry Norms:

Look at your return for capital invested against industry benchmarks. Understanding how your mission performs comparative with industry midpoints gives setting and recognizes regions for development.

All in all, powerful planning and fastidious following of return on initial capital investment are essential for fruitful virtual entertainment promoting efforts. In order to keep up with the ever-changing nature of digital marketing, businesses must adjust their resource allocation and continuously improve their strategies based on performance data. By incorporating these practices, organizations can not just explore the intricacies of web-based entertainment publicizing yet in addition drive significant and quantifiable outcomes.

Setting Advertising Budgets

Setting promoting spending plans is a basic part of any business' showcasing methodology. It includes deciding the monetary assignment for limited time exercises to accomplish explicit showcasing goals. When determining advertising budgets, a thoughtful approach is necessary to ensure that marketing efforts have the greatest impact possible.

Businesses must first take into account their overall marketing goals. What do they hope to accomplish with their advertising? Whether it's rising image mindfulness, driving deals, or sending off another item, having clear goals gives a structure to spending plan designation. For example, an item send off might require a more significant financial plan to produce introductory buzz and draw in a huge crowd.

Understanding the interest group is another pivotal element. Various socioeconomics and market fragments might answer diversely to different publicizing channels. Exploring and distinguishing the inclinations and ways of behaving of the main interest group help in choosing the best and cost-proficient publicizing mediums. Virtual entertainment stages may be more reasonable for contacting a more youthful crowd, while customary media like TV and radio may be better for a more seasoned segment.

The serious scene likewise assumes a crucial part in financial plan assurance. It is possible to gain insight into the standards and expectations of the industry by analyzing the advertising strategies utilized by competitors. A company may decide to devote additional resources to a particular channel as a result of competitors investing heavily in that channel. Going against the norm, finding undiscovered or less-investigated channels can introduce open doors for savvy publicizing.

Businesses must evaluate their overall financial situation after taking into consideration their objectives, target audience, and competitive analysis. The publicizing spending plan necessitates to line up with the organization's monetary abilities. Independent ventures could have more restricted assets contrasted with bigger undertakings, so they should zero in on savvy systems. Alternately, bigger organizations could have greater adaptability however need to guarantee that the financial plan lines up with the normal returns.

The planning of promoting efforts is likewise basic. Irregularity, item dispatches, or explicit occasions can impact when to dispense more spending plan to publicizing. During the holiday season, for instance, a retail business might increase its budget to take advantage of increased consumer spending. Campaigns that are designed around these shifts are more likely to resonate with their intended audience and use resources effectively.

Profit from speculation (return for capital invested) is a key measurement in deciding the viability of publicizing endeavors. The effectiveness of campaigns should be continuously evaluated and monitored by businesses. Assuming a specific channel or technique is conveying a high return for capital invested, it might legitimize dispensing a bigger piece of the financial plan to that area. Routinely evaluating the return for money invested considers dexterity in redistributing assets in view of what is working best.

Testing and trial and error are indispensable to enhancing promoting spending plans. A/B testing different promotion creatives, messages, and channels can give significant experiences into what resounds most with the crowd. Businesses can fine-tune their strategies using this iterative approach, ensuring that the campaign's budget is spent on the most effective components.

In the computerized age, information examination assumes a critical part in directing publicizing financial plan choices. Following measurements, for example, navigate rates, change rates, and commitment levels gives continuous input on the exhibition of missions. Businesses can quickly adjust their strategies and make informed decisions about how to allocate their budgets thanks to analytics tools.

Adaptability is a critical guideline in setting publicizing spending plans. Economic situations, customer ways of behaving, and cutthroat scenes can change quickly. Organizations should be dexterous in changing their financial plans to adjust to these changes. Having an adaptable planning approach considers speedy reactions to unexpected conditions or open doors on the lookout.

All in all, setting publicizing spending plans is an essential cycle that includes adjusting goals, figuring out the interest group, examining contenders, taking into account monetary capacities, and persistently observing execution. It requires a harmony between distributing adequate assets to accomplish promoting objectives and guaranteeing cost-viability. Businesses can maximize the impact of their advertising budgets in a dynamic and competitive market by employing a data-driven and adaptable strategy.

Calculating Return on Investment

Return on Investment (ROI) is a crucial financial metric used to evaluate the profitability and efficiency of an investment. It provides a standardized way to assess the performance of various investments, enabling individuals and businesses to make informed decisions about allocating resources. Calculating ROI involves comparing the gain or loss generated from an investment relative to its cost. This ratio is expressed as a percentage, making it easier to interpret and compare across different investment opportunities.

The basic formula for ROI is:

ROI =

Current Value of Investment−Cost of Investment

$$(\frac{\text{\textemdash\textemdash\textemdash\textemdash\textemdash\textemdash\textemdash\textemdash\textemdash}}{})$$

Cost of Investment

100

This simple formula encapsulates the essence of ROI, representing the percentage increase or decrease in the value of an investment relative to its initial cost. Let's delve deeper into the components of this formula and explore how to apply it in various scenarios.

Understanding the Components:

Current Value of Investment:

This refers to the present value of the investment, which includes any income, interest, or appreciation gained over time.

For example, if you initially invested $10,000 in stocks and the current value is $15,000, the current value of your investment is $15,000

.

Cost of Investment:

This represents the initial amount invested, encompassing the purchase price, transaction fees, and any additional costs associated with acquiring the investment.

In the example above, if the initial investment was $10,000, then the cost of investment is $10,000.

Practical Application:

Consider a real estate investment where an individual purchases a property for $200,000. Over the next five years, they make improvements worth $50,000, bringing the total cost to $250,000. After this period, they sell the property for $350,000. To calculate the

ROI=

Current Value of Investment−Cost of Investment

(--
--------------)

Cost of Investment

100

ROI=(

$350,000−$250,000$250,000)×100

$250,000

40%

The positive 40% ROI indicates a profitable investment. For every dollar invested, there was a 40% return.

Significance of ROI:

Comparative Analysis:

ROI allows investors to compare the performance of different investments on a standardized scale. It helps in prioritizing and selecting the most lucrative opportunities.

Decision-Making Tool:

Businesses use ROI to assess the viability of projects or initiatives. By comparing potential returns with costs, they can make strategic decisions on resource allocation.

Performance Evaluation:

Investors and portfolio managers use ROI to evaluate the performance of their investment portfolios. It aids in identifying underperforming assets and making adjustments.

Risk Assessment:

ROI is a valuable tool for assessing the risk associated with an investment. A higher ROI may indicate higher potential returns but could also come with increased risk.

Limitations of ROI:

Time Frame Consideration:

ROI doesn't account for the time it takes to realize returns. Two investments with the same ROI may have different payback periods, impacting liquidity.

Ignoring External Factors:

External factors such as economic conditions, market trends, and regulatory changes can influence an investment's performance, but ROI doesn't capture these nuances.

Neglecting Intangible Benefits:

ROI focuses on tangible returns and may overlook intangible benefits like brand reputation or employee satisfaction, which can be critical for businesses.

Calculating Return on Investment is a fundamental financial practice that empowers individuals and businesses to make informed financial decisions. It provides a standardized metric for evaluating the success of investments, aiding in comparative analysis, strategic planning, and risk assessment. However, it's essential to recognize the limitations of ROI and consider additional factors when making complex investment decisions. By understanding and effectively applying ROI, investors can navigate the dynamic landscape of financial markets and optimize their resource allocation for maximum returns.

Chapter 5
Emerging Trends in Social Media Advertising

Online entertainment publicizing has developed fundamentally throughout the long term, changing into a dynamic and powerful power in the promoting scene. As innovation keeps on progressing, recent fads arise, reshaping the manner in which organizations associate with their interest group. In this quickly evolving climate, keeping up to date with arising patterns is essential for advertisers trying to improve their methodologies and remain in front of the opposition.

Extended Reality (AR) and Expanded Reality (VR) Joining:

Increased and augmented reality have entered the virtual entertainment promoting domain, giving vivid encounters to clients. Brands are utilizing AR channels and VR content to draw in crowds in extraordinary and intelligent ways. This pattern improves client commitment as well as permits buyers to encounter items or administrations prior to settling on a buy choice.

Short-Structure Video Strength:
The ascent of short-structure video content on stages like TikTok and Instagram Reels has turned into a prevailing power in web-based entertainment promoting. Brands are profiting by the pattern by making appealing and brief recordings to catch the consideration of clients with contracting capacities to focus. These stages offer imaginative material for advertisers to pass on messages really in practically no time.

Vaporous Substance:
Stories on stages like Instagram, Snapchat, and Facebook have acquired gigantic prevalence. A sense of urgency and exclusivity are created by ephemeral content, which disappears after a predetermined amount of time. Advertisers are using this pattern to convey time-delicate advancements, in the background content, and sneak looks, cultivating a continuous association with the crowd.

Force to be reckoned with Promoting Development:
Powerhouse promoting has developed past simple supports, with forces to be reckoned with becoming fundamental associates in brand crusades. Miniature and nano powerhouses, with more modest but exceptionally drawn in followings, are gaining momentum as they offer more true associations with their crowd. Additionally, artificial intelligence (AI) is increasingly being used to select the ideal influencers for particular campaigns.

Social Business Reconciliation:
The distinction between discovery and purchase is becoming increasingly

muddled on social media platforms. Highlights like Instagram Shopping and Facebook Commercial center permit clients to investigate and purchase items without leaving the application. Social business is reforming the internet shopping experience, giving a consistent excursion from item disclosure to buy straightforwardly inside the virtual entertainment environment.

Personalization Fueled by simulated intelligence:

Man-made consciousness is assuming a vital part in upgrading the personalization of web-based entertainment promoting. Artificial intelligence calculations dissect client conduct, inclinations, and socioeconomics to convey custom fitted substance and ads. This degree of personalization further develops client experience as well as expands the viability of promotion crusades by focusing on the right crowd with pertinent substance.

Intelligent Substance Configurations:

Commitment is key in virtual entertainment, and intuitive substance designs like surveys, tests, and intuitive stories are acquiring notoriety. These organizations support client investment, giving a two-way correspondence channel among brands and their crowd. Advertisers are utilizing intuitive substance to accumulate important bits of knowledge, improve brand review, and make significant encounters.

Client Created Content Enhancement:

Client created content (UGC) keeps on being an integral asset in web-based entertainment publicizing. Brands are empowering their clients to make content connected with their items or administrations, utilizing the validity and trust related with peer proposals. Reusing UGC in promotion crusades helps construct a feeling of locality and encourages an association between the brand and its crowd.

Moral and Socially Capable Promoting:

Buyers are progressively esteeming brands that line up with their qualities. Brands are incorporating socially and ethically responsible messaging into their social media advertisements to reflect this shift. Advertisers are recognizing the significance of creating a positive brand image that resonates with consumers who are socially conscious in a variety of contexts, including diversity and inclusion initiatives and sustainability initiatives.

Regulations and Concerns About Data Privacy:

As the consciousness of information protection develops, virtual entertainment stages are confronting expanded examination. To protect user data, new trends include stricter regulations like the GDPR and CCPA. Advertisers need to explore this scene cautiously, guaranteeing consistency with guidelines while keeping up with compelling focusing on systems.

Taking everything into account, the scene of virtual entertainment publicizing is constantly advancing, introducing the two difficulties and valuable open doors for advertisers. Remaining informed about arising patterns is fundamental for making systems that reverberate with the constantly changing inclinations of buyers. Whether through vivid advances, short-structure recordings, or moral promoting rehearses, the fate of virtual entertainment publicizing guarantees development and versatility to fulfill the needs of a powerful computerized scene.

New Features and Tools

Web-based entertainment publicizing has seen a quick development lately, determined by the consistently changing scene of computerized showcasing. With the persistent development of new highlights and apparatuses, online entertainment stages are furnishing sponsors with imaginative ways of interfacing with their ideal interest groups. Not only do these advancements improve the advertising experience as a whole, but they also contribute to the effectiveness of campaigns. In this investigation, we will dive into a few essential new highlights and devices that are reshaping the domain of virtual entertainment publicizing.

One unmistakable pattern is the ascent of expanded reality (AR) in web-based entertainment promoting. Facebook and Instagram have introduced augmented reality (AR) features that let users virtually interact with products. Advertisers can use augmented reality (AR) to create immersive experiences that let customers see products in their actual environments before making a purchase. This upgrades client commitment as well as helps in conquering the limits of web based shopping by giving a more unmistakable encounter.

Another game-changing expansion is the mix of man-made reasoning (artificial intelligence) in online entertainment publicizing. Man-made intelligence calculations currently power progressed focusing on abilities, empowering sponsors to arrive at explicit socioeconomics with accuracy. AI calculations investigate client conduct, interests, and commitment examples to enhance promotion conveyance. This works on the pertinence of promotions as well as improves generally crusade execution by boosting reach and commitment.

Video content keeps on overwhelming the web-based entertainment scene, and stages are continually acquainting highlights with enhancing the video promoting experience. Video-integrated interactive elements like polls, quizzes, and shoppable tags are becoming increasingly popular. The likelihood of audience retention and conversion is increased by these features, which transform passive viewers into active participants. Moreover, the ascent of live video web based offers a constant association among brands and their crowd, cultivating realness and promptness in promoting endeavors.

Fleeting substance, described by its transitory nature, has turned into an amazing asset in online entertainment promotion. Stories on stages like Instagram, Snapchat, and Facebook have become key parts of publicizing methodologies. Promoters can use stories to make a need to get going, restrictiveness, and realness. The transient idea of this content lines up with the more limited focusing ability of current buyers, making it a successful method for passing on messages rapidly and compellingly.

Social business is another change in perspective in the realm of virtual entertainment publicizing. Shopping features are being integrated directly into the user experience on platforms. Clients can now find, investigate, and buy items without leaving the web-based entertainment application. Shoppable posts and in-application checkout choices smooth out the buy cycle, lessening erosion for purchasers and furnishing publicists with a consistent way to transformation. The consumer journey is being reshaped by this convergence of social media and e-commerce, providing advertisers with new opportunities to capitalize on impulse purchases.

Powerhouse promoting stays a strong power in online entertainment publicizing, and stages are acquainted with highlights with improved coordinated effort among brands and forces to be reckoned with. Instruments that work with powerhouse disclosure, execution following, and content endorsement smooth out the coordinated effort process. Brands can now distinguish powerhouses whose crowd lines up with their objective socioeconomics, measure the effect of force to be reckoned with crusades, and keep up with command over the information related with their image.

The significance of information security and client agreement has prompted the execution of stricter guidelines and upgraded client controls via virtual entertainment stages. Publicists are adjusting to these progressions by focusing on straightforwardness and assent driven approaches. Highlights that permit clients to control the information they share and the advertisements they see are becoming norm. Publicists need to explore this scene dependably, regarding client security while conveying customized and important substance.

cutting-edge tools and features continue to shape the ever-evolving advertising landscape on social media. From expanded reality and computerized reasoning to intuitive recordings and social trade, these headways enable promoters to make seriously captivating and customized encounters for their crowd. As the business keeps on advancing, keeping up to date with these advancements will be pivotal for publicists looking to amplify the effect of their virtual entertainment crusades.

Adaptation to Algorithm Changes

Variation to calculation changes is a vital part of exploring the consistently developing scene of computerized stages. Algorithms are the foundation of search engines, social media platforms, and a variety of online services in the fast-paced world of technology. These calculations go through consistent updates and changes, introducing difficulties and open doors for people and organizations the same.

One of the essential purposes for calculation changes is the quest for further developed client experience. Advanced stages continually endeavor to improve the significance and nature of content introduced to clients. This goal prompts algorithmic changes that consider client conduct, inclinations, and arising patterns. As a result, anyone aiming to maintain or enhance their online visibility must keep up with these changes.

Google's search engine algorithms, for example, are notorious for their frequent updates. These changes can essentially affect site rankings, impacting the progression of natural traffic. In order to keep up with the most recent requirements, businesses and website owners must be proactive in monitoring algorithmic changes and adapting their strategies.

Content makers, for example, need to remain watchful about watchword patterns and search aims. Calculation changes frequently focus on a great, applicable substance that offers some benefit to clients. Making content that resounds with interest groups and complies with the most recent Web optimization rules becomes central. This might include streamlining for voice search, grasping semantic hunt, and making content that lines up with the ebb and flow positioning variables.

Web-based entertainment stages additionally constantly change their calculations to refine content conveyance to clients. People and businesses that use social media for promotion need to be flexible in how they adjust their strategies because these changes affect how visible posts are. Connecting with content, true collaborations, and a comprehension of the stage explicit calculations become fundamental to keeping major areas of strength for a presence.

Also, the ascent of algorithmic powerhouses in the online entertainment domain adds one more layer of intricacy. These powerhouses influence calculations to amplify their scope and commitment. Adjusting to these progressions includes grasping the subtleties of every stage, trying different things with content configurations, and developing a veritable association with the crowd.

Web based business organizations, subject to stages like Amazon, wrestle with algorithmic movements that impact item rankings. Remaining cutthroat requires a profound comprehension of the variables impacting these rankings, for example, client surveys, item depictions, and estimating techniques. Customary acclimations to publicizing and limited time exercises are important to line up with the stage's advancing calculations.

In the domain of computerized showcasing, the transformation reaches out to paid promotion. Stages like Facebook and Google Promotions regularly update their calculations to streamline advertisement conveyance and improve client experience. Promoters should stay light-footed in changing, focusing on boundaries, advertisement creatives, and offering procedures to line up with these changes. The capacity to decipher examination information becomes significant for refining efforts in light of moving algorithmic scenes.

Also, calculation changes frequently brief changes in purchaser conduct. For example, changes in web crawler calculations might impact how clients find and cooperate with content. Understanding these conduct shifts is imperative for organizations hoping to tailor their methodologies to developing buyer inclinations. Adjusting to these progressions might include reexamining showcasing messages, changing item situating, or investigating new channels to arrive at the ideal interest group.

All in all, transformation to calculation changes is a powerful cycle that traverses different parts of the computerized scene. Whether exploring web index refreshes, online entertainment calculation changes, or online business stage movements, people and organizations should stay careful and coordinated. Not only is it a defensive measure, but it is also a proactive strategy for staying ahead of the competition in the online environment by comprehending and implementing strategies that are in line with the most recent algorithmic requirements. Fruitful transformation includes consistent learning, trial and error, and a readiness to embrace change chasing supported computerized pertinence.

Chapter 6
Case Studies and Successful Campaigns on Each Platform

Online entertainment publicizing has turned into a fundamental piece of computerized showcasing, furnishing organizations with an incredible asset to arrive at their ideal interest group. Fruitful missions on stages like Facebook, Instagram, and LinkedIn frequently depend on essential preparation, convincing substance, and grasping the exceptional elements of every stage.

Facebook:

Facebook stays a juggernaut in the virtual entertainment promoting scene, flaunting over 2.8 billion month to month dynamic clients. Facebook's extensive targeting options are frequently used in profitable campaigns. One remarkable contextual investigation is the "Offer a Coke" crusade by Coca-Cola. The organization customized its advertisements by including individual names on Coke bottles, empowering clients to share photographs of their customized bottles. The mission drove commitment as well as made a feeling of special interaction with the brand. Utilizing client produced content, Coca-Cola transformed shoppers into brand envoys. The progress of this mission features the viability of personalization and client inclusion on Facebook.

Instagram:

Instagram is a one-of-a-kind platform for brands to showcase their goods or services because of its emphasis on visuals. The stage has more than 1 billion month to month dynamic clients, setting aside it a significant room for organizations to interface with an outwardly situated crowd. A phenomenal illustration of a fruitful Instagram crusade is Nike's #AirMaxDay.

Nike profited by the yearly festival of its famous Air Max shoes by making an outwardly shocking and vivid mission on Instagram. The campaign became a global celebration as the brand encouraged users to share their own Air Max photos using the hashtag. By taking advantage of the client created content pattern, Nike fortified its relationship with existing clients as well as contacted new crowds through the legitimate substance shared by clients.

LinkedIn:

LinkedIn, known for its proficient concentration, offers an exceptional space for B2B showcasing and proficient systems administration. One outstanding illustration is Microsoft's "Inclusion Starts with I" campaign. Microsoft utilized LinkedIn to elevate its obligation to variety and incorporation, sharing accounts of representatives and underlining the significance of cultivating a comprehensive work environment. By lining up with LinkedIn's expert ethos and tending to a socially significant subject, Microsoft effectively drew in the stage's business-situated crowd. This mission outlines the significance of fitting substance to the stage's particular crowd and values, exhibiting how LinkedIn can be an incredible asset for advancing corporate social obligation.

Cross-Stage Systems:

Even though each platform has its advantages, effective social media advertising frequently requires a unified approach across multiple platforms. A prominent model is Airbnb's "Live There" crusade. The idea of experiencing a city like a local rather than a tourist was promoted by the company through a combination of Facebook, Instagram, and Twitter.

By modifying content for every stage while keeping a reliable message, Airbnb really contacted different crowds across virtual entertainment. This mission highlights the significance of figuring out the special qualities of every stage and fitting substance likewise, guaranteeing an agreeable and effective cross-stage presence.

Key Success Strategies:
Crowd Focusing on:

Comprehend your main interest group and influence the definite focusing on choices given by every stage.Utilize segment, interest, and social information to make customized crusades.

Attractive Visuals:

Create content that is visually appealing and shareable to take advantage of the visual nature of social media platforms.

In a crowded online space, invest in high-quality images and videos to attract users' attention.

Client Created Content:
Users should be encouraged to produce and share content about your brand.

Client produced content adds legitimacy and can transform clients into brand advocates.

Stage Explicit Substance:
Tailor your substance to fit the interesting attributes and client assumptions for every stage.

Figure out the tone, style, and content inclinations of the crowd on every stage.

Information Investigation:
Routinely dissect execution measurements to survey the progress of your missions.Utilize data to fine-tune strategies, enhance targeting, and enhance the overall efficacy of a campaign.

All in all, fruitful online entertainment promotion requires a profound comprehension of every stage, a fitted way to deal with content creation, and a guarantee to draw in with the crowd legitimately. By gaining from these contextual analyses and consolidating key systems, organizations can explore the powerful scene of online entertainment publicizing and accomplish significant outcomes.

Chapter 7
Pitfalls to
Avoid

Crafting successful social media advertising campaigns can be a powerful tool for businesses, but navigating this dynamic landscape comes with its fair share of pitfalls. Avoiding these traps is crucial to maximize the effectiveness of your efforts. Let's explore some common pitfalls and strategies to sidestep them.

1. Ignoring Audience Targeting:

One of the biggest mistakes in social media advertising is neglecting the importance of precise audience targeting. Casting too wide a net can lead to wasted resources and missed opportunities. Define your target audience based on demographics, interests, and behaviors to ensure your ads reach the right people.

2. Neglecting Platform-Specific Strategies:

Each social media platform has its unique characteristics and user behavior. A one-size-fits-all approach won't cut it. Tailor your content and strategy for each platform. What works on Instagram may not resonate on LinkedIn. Understand the strengths and limitations of each platform to optimize your advertising strategy accordingly.

3. Overlooking Ad Creativity:
In the fast-paced world of social media, dull and uninspiring content gets scrolled past quickly. Invest time and resources in creating visually appealing and engaging ads. Utilize eye-catching images or videos, compelling headlines, and concise, relevant copy to capture attention within seconds.

4. Neglecting Mobile Optimization:
With the majority of social media users accessing platforms on mobile devices, failing to optimize your ads for mobile can be a costly mistake. Ensure that your visuals, text, and overall layout are mobile-friendly to deliver a seamless experience across all devices.

5. Ignoring Analytics:
Neglecting to analyze the performance of your social media ads is a surefire way to miss out on optimization opportunities. Regularly monitor key metrics such as click-through rates, conversion rates, and engagement. Use this data to refine your strategy, focusing on what works and eliminating what doesn't.

6. Overlooking A/B Testing:
A/B testing is a powerful tool to fine-tune your social media ads. Testing different elements like headlines, visuals, or calls-to-action allows you to identify the most effective combinations. Regularly experiment with variations to optimize your campaigns over time.

7. Failing to Set Clear Objectives:
Without clear goals, it's challenging to measure the success of your social media advertising efforts. Define

specific, measurable objectives, whether it's brand awareness, lead generation, or sales. Align your ad content and strategy with these objectives to drive meaningful results.

8. Ignoring Negative Feedback:

Social media provides a platform for users to express their opinions, and negative feedback is inevitable. Ignoring or dismissing criticism can harm your brand reputation. Instead, address negative comments professionally and use them as an opportunity to learn and improve.

9. Being Inconsistent:

Consistency is key in social media advertising. A sporadic posting schedule or inconsistent brand messaging can confuse your audience. Establish a consistent posting frequency and maintain a cohesive brand voice across all platforms for a stronger brand identity.

10. Relying Solely on Paid Ads:

(vbnet Copy code)

While paid ads are essential, relying solely on them can limit your reach. Incorporate organic strategies like regular posts, user-generated content, and community engagement. A balanced approach ensures a more holistic and sustainable presence on social media.

11. Ignoring Trends and Algorithm Changes:

(css code)

Social media platforms frequently update their algorithms and introduce new features. Staying oblivious to these changes can hinder your visibility. Stay informed about industry trends and platform updates to adapt your strategy accordingly.

12. Setting and Forgetting:

(vbnet code)

Social media advertising requires ongoing attention and adjustments. Don't set up your campaigns and forget about them. Regularly review and optimize your ads based on performance metrics, audience feedback, and changes in your business objectives.

13. Neglecting Customer Engagement:

(vbnet code)

Social media is a two-way street. Failing to engage with your audience can make your brand seem distant and unapproachable. Respond to comments, messages, and mentions promptly. Foster a sense of community by actively participating in conversations.

14. Ignoring Privacy Concerns:

(vbnet code)

With increasing awareness of privacy issues, users are more cautious about sharing personal information. Be transparent about how you use customer data and comply with privacy regulations. Building trust is crucial for long-term success.

15. Lack of Adaptability:

(csharp code)

Social media is a dynamic environment. What worked yesterday may not work tomorrow. Stay adaptable and be ready to pivot your strategy based on changing market trends, user behavior, and platform updates.

By steering clear of these pitfalls and adopting a strategic, adaptable approach, your social media advertising efforts can yield more significant and sustainable results. Regularly reassess your strategy, stay informed about industry trends, and prioritize audience engagement to build a successful and enduring social media presence.

Common Mistakes in Social Media Advertising

Negative Impacts on Brand Reputation

Adverse consequences on brand notoriety can have broad ramifications for organizations, influencing their primary concern, client trust, and long haul achievement. A damaged reputation can spread rapidly and be difficult to recover from in today's interconnected world, where information moves quickly through various online platforms.

A public relations crisis is a significant contributor to brand reputation damage. Incidents like product recalls, data breaches, and scandals involving company executives all have the potential to rapidly undermine consumer trust. The manner in which a brand handles these emergencies is significant in deciding the degree of the harm. Inability to answer speedily, straightforwardly, and really can bring about enduring mischief to the brand's picture.

Online entertainment enhances the effect of adverse occasions, as news gets out quickly and conversations become viral. Clients share their perspectives, and negative feelings can pick up speed, contacting a tremendous crowd. Brands should effectively screen and deal with their web-based presence to resolve issues speedily and alleviate expected harm.

Reviews and comments left by customers also have a significant impact on how people perceive a brand. Negative surveys, particularly when various or exceptionally noticeable, can impact expected clients' choices. Brands that disregard to address client concerns or give lacking arrangements risk estranging their client base and hurting their standing. Then again, answering emphatically and settling issues can exhibit a promise to consumer loyalty and assist with reconstructing trust.

Deceptive strategic policies can have extreme repercussions on brand notoriety. Customers' credibility and trust can be damaged by cases of fraud, dishonesty, or exploitation. The general population is progressively esteeming straightforwardness and moral way of behaving, and any deviation from these standards can bring about long haul harm to a brand's standing.

Ecological and social obligations have become basic elements in forming brand discernment. Shoppers are progressively aware of the effect organizations have on the climate and society. Brands that disregard these contemplations or participate in exercises apparent as unsafe can confront kickback, adversely influencing their standing. On the other hand, businesses that place a high value on social responsibility and sustainability have a better chance of attracting customers who care about the environment.

Representative related issues can likewise add to a negative brand picture. Occasions of work environment badgering, separation, or uncalled for work practices can discolor a brand's standing. Besides, how an organization answers such issues, including its obligation to resolving inner issues, influences outside discernments. Brands that encourage a positive and comprehensive work environment culture are bound to be seen well by the two representatives and people in general.

Cutthroat tensions and market elements can likewise prompt brand notoriety challenges. Bogus or misdirecting examinations with contenders, forceful promoting strategies, or endeavors to control popular assessment can misfire and harm a brand's believability. Customers value validness, and any apparent scarcity in that department can bring about a deficiency of trust.

Legitimate issues, for example, claims or administrative infringement, represent a critical danger to mark notoriety. Cases including extortion, wellbeing concerns, or resistance with industry guidelines can have enduring outcomes.

Regardless of whether a brand in the long run wins in fights in court, the negative exposure during the cycle can hurt its picture.

Taking everything into account, adverse consequences on brand notoriety can originate from different sources, including advertising emergencies, client criticism, dishonest practices, natural and social obligation issues, worker related issues, serious tensions, and legitimate difficulties. In the present interconnected and data driven climate, brands must proactively deal with their standing, answer really to issues, and focus on moral strategic policies to assemble and keep up with entrust with shoppers. A damaged reputation has far-reaching effects that can have a significant impact on a brand's market success and longevity.

Chapter 8 Future Outlook

Web-based entertainment promotion is ready for huge development before long, with a few key patterns molding its future viewpoint. As innovation proceeds to progress and purchaser conduct develops, sponsors should adjust to remain applicable and viable in this unique scene.

One significant pattern that is probably going to shape the fate of web-based entertainment publicizing is the expanded reconciliation of man-made reasoning (artificial intelligence) and AI (ML) calculations. These innovations engage publicists to make more customized and designated crusades of information. Man-made intelligence calculations can anticipate client conduct, inclinations, and commitment designs, permitting publicists to fit their substance to explicit crowds.

Besides, man-made intelligence driven chatbots are turning into an essential part of web-based entertainment publicizing. Brands are utilizing chatbots to draw in with clients continuously, giving moment reactions to requests and conveying customized content. This upgrades client experience as well as permits promoters to accumulate significant bits of knowledge into customer inclinations.

One more key part representing things to come of virtual entertainment publicizing is the developing accentuation on force to be reckoned with advertising. Powerhouses, people with a significant following via online entertainment stages, have become strong brand advocates. Promoters are progressively teaming up with powerhouses to arrive at their main interest group in a more genuine and engaging manner. As buyers request legitimacy, powerhouse promoting offers a more veritable association among brands and their crowd.

Video content is expected to assume a vital part in store for web-based entertainment publicizing. Short-structure recordings, live streaming, and intuitive substance are acquiring notoriety across different stages.

Promoters should adjust their procedures to integrate outwardly engaging and connecting with video content to catch the consideration of clients looking at their feeds. Also, expanded reality (AR) and computer generated reality (VR) advancements might turn out to be more pervasive in virtual entertainment promoting, offering vivid and intelligent encounters for clients.

Another trend that will influence advertising on social media platforms in the future is the rise of social commerce. As stages like Instagram and Facebook keep on coordinating internet business highlights, promoters can consistently direct clients from item disclosure to buy inside a similar stage. Social commerce makes it easier for customers to shop because it blurs the lines between advertising and shopping.

Information security concerns have become progressively noticeable as of late, provoking changes in guidelines and client assumptions. Publicists should explore these worries cautiously and focus on straightforward and moral practices. The fate of virtual entertainment promotion will probably include stricter guidelines on information utilization, expecting publicists to focus on client security while as yet conveying designated and powerful missions.

The idea of social obligation is getting some decent forward movement, and purchasers are turning out to be more aware of the qualities and morals of the brands they support. Promoters should adjust their informing to social and natural causes to construct trust and resound with socially cognizant crowds.

Brands that exhibit a guarantee to positive social effect might acquire an upper hand in the packed online entertainment scene.

As far as stage inclinations, the scene might keep on moving. New stages might arise, and existing ones might advance or decrease in prominence. Promoters ought to remain coordinated and be prepared to adjust their systems in view of the stages generally applicable to their ideal interest group. As client socioeconomics change and new advancements arise, the viability of publicizing on unambiguous stages might fluctuate.

The fate of web-based entertainment publicizing is without a doubt intriguing and dynamic. Adverts must embrace technological advancements, comprehend shifting consumer behaviors, and implement novel strategies to stay ahead of the curve. Artificial intelligence and AI will assume a critical part in customizing and improving efforts, while powerhouse promoting, video content, social business, and an emphasis on friendly obligation will shape the story of virtual entertainment publicizing in the years to come. As the scene keeps on developing, versatility and imagination will be key for sponsors trying to have a significant effect in the cutthroat universe of virtual entertainment publicizing.

Predictions for the Evolution of Social Media Advertising

Virtual entertainment publicizing has gone through huge changes as of late, and its development is ready to keep molding the advanced advertising scene. As we look forward, a few patterns and expectations arise, illustrating the likely direction of online entertainment publicizing.

Personalization's rise:

Personalization has turned into a foundation of successful publicizing, and web-based entertainment stages are supposed to use client information for additional custom fitted missions progressively. Promoters will probably utilize progressed calculations to break down client conduct, inclinations, and socioeconomics to convey customized content, improving client commitment and transformation rates.

Increased Reality (AR) Mix:

It is anticipated that the use of augmented reality in social media advertising will expand. AR encounters, for example, virtual attempts or intelligent promotions, can possibly give clients vivid and connected content, making a more noteworthy and shareable publicizing experience.

Video Prevalence:

Video content has been acquiring unmistakable quality in online entertainment, and this pattern is supposed to escalate. Short-structure recordings, live web based, and intuitive video promotions will probably rule online entertainment stages, offering publicists different and drawing in organizations to associate with their crowd.

Vaporous Substance Development:
Transient substance, described by its transitory nature, is on the ascent. Stories on stages like Instagram and Snapchat have acquired enormous ubiquity. This trend is likely to be capitalized on by advertisers, who will produce limited-time, time-sensitive content that creates a sense of urgency and exclusivity and encourages user engagement.

Maturity in Influencer Marketing:
It is anticipated that influencer marketing will mature and become more sophisticated. Publicists will probably zero in on long haul associations with powerhouses who adjust intimately with their image values. Miniature and nano-powerhouses may likewise acquire unmistakable quality as brands look for more credible and specialty associations with their interest group.

Social Trade Development:
Web-based entertainment stages are progressively becoming shopping objections. The mix of web based business includes straightforwardly inside stages empowers clients to make buys without leaving the application. With platforms constantly improving their shopping features and advertisers optimizing for seamless transactions, this trend is likely to grow.

Concerns About Privacy and Regulation:
The development of virtual entertainment promoting won't be

without challenges. Administrative examination and security concerns will probably shape the scene. To build and maintain user trust, advertisers will need to navigate changing privacy regulations and implement transparent practices.

Optimization based on artificial intelligence (AI):

Optimizing advertising campaigns on social media will rely heavily on AI. From chatbots for client communication to simulated intelligence driven promotion focusing on and execution examination, the incorporation of computerized reasoning is set to smooth out processes, improve productivity, and convey more compelling publicizing results.

Intuitive Substance and Gamification:

Intelligent substance and gamification components will probably turn out to be more predominant in virtual entertainment publicizing. Drawing in clients through tests, surveys, and games can make a feeling of support, making the promotion experience more charming and essential.

Cross-Stage Coordination:

Promoters are supposed to progressively use cross-stage methodologies to contact a more extensive crowd. Consistent coordination across different web-based entertainment stages, combined with steady informing, will become significant for a firm and powerful publicizing procedure.

Measurements Development:

The measurements used to quantify the outcome of online entertainment promotion are probably going to develop. Past conventional measurements like snaps and impressions, there will be a more noteworthy accentuation on estimating significant commitment, change attribution, and the general effect on brand discernment.

All in all, the development of online entertainment promoting is set apart by a shift towards more customized, vivid, and intuitive encounters. Sponsors should remain spry, adjusting to innovative headways, administrative changes, and moving customer ways of behaving. Advertisers' methods for meaningfully connecting with their target audience will also continue to evolve alongside social media platforms. The eventual fate of web-based entertainment publicizing guarantees development, innovativeness, and a profound reconciliation of computerized showcasing into the texture of our internet based connections.

CONCLUSIO N

Recap of Strategies on Encouragement for Ongoing Adaptation and Innovation

All in all, the scene of web-based entertainment promotion is dynamic and always advancing, requesting ceaseless variation and advancement. The techniques utilized to energize continuous transformation and development in this domain are multi-layered, enveloping different parts of content creation, crowd commitment, and mechanical reconciliation.

One key technique is the accentuation of information driven navigation. As web-based entertainment stages become progressively complex in their information examination abilities, promoters can use these bits of knowledge to refine and upgrade their missions. By intently observing measurements, for example, commitment rates, navigate rates, and change information, sponsors can acquire significant bits of knowledge into crowd inclinations and ways of behaving. Real-time adjustments are made possible by this data-driven strategy, ensuring that campaigns remain relevant and effective in the face of shifting market trends.

Besides, cultivating a culture of imagination is fundamental for continuous variation and development in virtual entertainment publicizing. Empowering groups to consider some fresh possibilities, explore different avenues regarding new configurations, and push inventive limits can prompt advancement crusades that catch crowd consideration. Whether through outwardly staggering substance, intuitive encounters, or remarkable narrating, imaginative development stays a main impetus in keeping an upper hand in the consistently packed online entertainment scene.

Cooperation and cross-utilitarian collaboration likewise assume an urgent part in driving continuous variation and development. Web-based entertainment promoting is a multidisciplinary field that requires mastery in regions like showcasing, plan, information examination, and innovation. Uniting people with different ranges of abilities encourages a cooperative climate where thoughts can be shared, refined, and carried out flawlessly. This approach improves the nature of missions as well as works with the speedy combination of arising patterns and advances.

In addition, keeping up to date with mechanical progressions is critical for adjusting to the quickly changing scene of virtual entertainment publicizing. The incorporation of man-made reasoning, expanded reality, and other arising advancements can altogether upgrade the viability of missions. For example, man-made intelligence fueled calculations can enhance focusing on and personalization, guaranteeing that notices are conveyed to the most significant crowds. Embracing and integrating these innovative progressions empowers promoters to remain on the ball and keep an upper hand.

Notwithstanding mechanical headways, keeping a heartbeat on friendly and social trends is basic. Understanding the developing inclinations and ways of behaving of interest groups permits sponsors to in like manner tailor their systems. Web-based entertainment is an impression of cultural elements, and missions that reverberate with latest things and social subtleties are bound to catch crowd consideration and cultivate commitment. Routinely directing statistical surveying, observing virtual entertainment drifts, and remaining sensitive to social movements are basic parts of a proactive methodology for continuous transformation.

Moreover, the significance of encouraging significant communications couldn't possibly be more significant. Virtual entertainment stages are not simply channels for broadcasting promotions; they are intuitive spaces where brands can connect straightforwardly with their crowds. Constructing and sustaining connections through certified discussions, answering client remarks, and effectively partaking in important conversations add to a positive brand picture and encourage client reliability. This accentuation on credible commitment improves the adequacy of current missions as well as lays the basis for continuous variation in view of client criticism and inclinations.

The significance of agility in social media advertising must also be acknowledged. One of the hallmarks of successful campaigns is the capacity to quickly pivot in response to unanticipated difficulties or to take advantage of emerging opportunities. Adjusting to changes in calculations, stage strategies, or industry patterns requires a deft methodology. Laying out processes that consider quick navigation, execution, and streamlining is critical for keeping up with readiness in the speedy universe of online entertainment promotion.

All in all, the procedures for empowering continuous transformation and development in web-based entertainment promotion are interconnected and dynamic. From utilizing information driven bits of knowledge to cultivating a culture of inventiveness, embracing innovative headways, remaining sensitive to social patterns, encouraging significant corporations, and keeping up with dexterity — every part adds to an all encompassing methodology for exploring the developing scene of online entertainment publicizing. Sponsors who proactively embrace and coordinate these procedures into their missions are better situated to get by as well as flourish in the always impacting universe of online entertainment promoting.

DEAR READER

Your thoughts matter to us! if the book brought a smile or moment of respite, please Consider Sharing your experience through a review.

your feedback is invaluable in making our book even more enjoyable to following.We hope this message finds you well and enjoy your literary adventures! We value the opinions of our readers, and we would love to hear your thoughts on **(SOCIAL MEDIA ADVERTISING)**

Thank you for being a part of our literary journey, and we look forward to reading your review!

WARM REGARDS